S0-CFQ-118

Greetings from JANELAND

Women Write More About Leaving Men for Women

Edited by
Candace Walsh &
Barbara Straus Lodge

CLEiS
PRESS

Published in the United States by Cleis Press, an imprint of Start Midnight, LLC, 101 Hudson Street, Thirty-Seventh Floor, Suite 3705, Jersey City, NJ 07302.

Printed in the United States.
Cover design: Laura M. André
Cover photograph: Jenn Huls/Shutterstock.com
Text design: Frank Wiedemann
First Edition.
10 9 8 7 6 5 4 3 2 1

Trade paper ISBN: 978-1-62778-234-0
E-book ISBN: 978-1-62778-235-7

Library of Congress Cataloging-in-Publication Data is available on file.

Table of Contents

Foreword

BY TRISH BENDIX

FOR MOST OF MY ADULT CAREER, I HAVE WORKED AS A professional lesbian. It's been my job to immerse myself in lesbian culture and write about everything related to queer women in pop culture, entertainment, and the media.

I wasn't always so steeped in sapphic knowledge. Once upon a time, I assumed I was straight—but as a journalism student working at my college newspaper, I met and subsequently fell for my first girlfriend. Coming out in my early twenties was almost a surprise to me—I'd always assumed I was heterosexual, like I imagine, most people in my small hometown—but it also propelled me into a surprise career. I spent ten years working at AfterEllen, the largest website for LGBTQ women, where I had the opportunity to meet, work with, and detail the complex, diverse lives of queer women. And as I continue as editor in chief of *GO Magazine*, I can tell you confidently that the process of realizing one's sexuality is as different as the stars in our astrological charts. But we also share some common experiences—including that first time we start to question ourselves, sensing, perhaps unexpectedly, that we might not be 100 percent straight.

Some women know early—they can pinpoint preschool crushes on classmates and prepubescent desires for their P.E. teachers that clued them in they were different from the rest. But there are just as many, including me and the writers in this book, who were surprised by the appearance of an unanticipated sign. And when you realize something so significant about yourself after having heteronormative relationships, it's easy to ask yourself the invasive questions you'd never allow someone else to get away with: "How could I have not known?" Questions that insinuate you either knew and kept it a secret, or worse, are too daft to truly know something so integral to who you are.

Because, as most of us know, once you acknowledge that you are a woman who loves other women, a lot of things change, including how you see yourself and how other people see you. It's a new framework through which to view the world, which is, in many ways, as scary as it is exciting. When I shared my coming out story seven years ago in *Dear John, I Love Jane*, I detailed how I felt like a fraud among lesbians who acknowledged their homosexuality much sooner than I had. It was a deep insecurity I held, trying to prove myself to the community I joined.

Now, having spent more than a decade deeply entrenched in the lesbian community, I can confirm, dear reader, that there is no ideal time to truly become—or acknowledge—who you are, and any stigma that might have once accompanied being a "late in life lesbian" is fading with every story shared in both the private and public sphere.

In 2009, one year before *Dear John, I Love Jane* was published, *The Oprah Winfrey Show* dedicated a show to "Women Leaving Men for Other Women." Despite Oprah's best efforts as a long-time LGBTQ ally, the episode was very much about the secret lives the guests were leading; women who were on track to have the perfect existence (houses in the suburbs! children! charmed lives!) but couldn't resist temptation. What was seen only a handful of years ago as an illicit lust that demanded explanation is now perceived as less about vice—it never was about vice to the women living through such revelations—and more about a person's claiming of their own identity. Someone's sexual orientation, stagnant or otherwise, has become less of a stigma, an indication of their character or worse, self-sabotage. Rather, it's finally being recognized for what it is: self-exploration.

Less than a decade later, what seemed like a fascinating trend for celebrities has become more commonplace, and I believe that it's because of the openness of the women who contributed their experiences to the conversation. Public figures like Carlease Burke, Elizabeth Gilbert, Meredith Baxter, Maria Bello, Kelly McGillis, Cynthia Nixon, Tatum O'Neal, Kristen Stewart, and Wanda Sykes have all spoken publicly about how love has surprised them, how their feelings for another woman hadn't been particularly expected and snuck up on them in a way that was at once terrifying, exhilarating, and comforting. Yet their shifts have prompted think pieces and fascination from a world that still sees things as binary—straight or gay. Any inability to commit to one for the entirety of your lifetime is just too mind-boggling for other people to comprehend. It's important to remember that while it's so very kind of them to dedicate such time and energy to your sexual identity, their concern is more about themselves than it is about you.

In 2014, writer Lauren Morelli came out about leaving her husband for actress Samira Wiley in a piece she penned for *Mic*, titled "While Writing for *Orange Is the New Black*, I Realized I Am Gay." In it, she details how she'd previously assumed she wasn't a very sexual person and how childhood flirtation with other girls wasn't any indication to her that she'd be interested in women. And when she came out, she had been married for only a few months—happily, she'd thought, until she started to ask herself, "Am I gay?"

Coming out to yourself later in life is an experience not specific to actresses and authors, of course—but those people make headlines when they come out, and those headlines have gone from expressing shock and awe to serving as public celebrations or, in some cases, normalized nonchalance, all of which indicates that these kinds of announcements are becoming less about sensationalizing lesbian sex and sexuality, and more about acknowledging respected relationships.

What used to be a death knell for public figures—coming out at any point in one's career, generally after having had a publicly known relationship with a partner of the opposite sex—has ultimately shifted to being less of a scandal and more of a shrug.

It's incredible how much can change with time—especially if you measure it through public opinions and temperaments—and how society's shifts in a matter of years can feel like it took both seconds and centuries. In the last five years, attitudes and legislation around marriage equality in the United States have changed as much as they have in the last five decades. Despite the tragedies and hateful acts that are still part of American culture, homosexuality has never been more legally and culturally accepted. At the same time, those of us who cherish marriage equality and equal protection under the law have gone into a stunned, defensive crouch after the 2016 presidential election. The people who voted for Donald Trump and Mike Pence (many of them family members, coworkers, neighbors, and even friends) have shown us the limits and the myths of their acceptance. We—and other vulnerable groups—will be fighting to hold our ground instead of coasting toward more safety, tolerance, and freedom.

Much of our power to dissolve prejudice and bigotry is in the stories we as lesbian, gay, bisexual, trans, and queer people tell. The simple truths about ourselves and our lives can break through walls of rhetoric—because even the most disappointingly homophobic people are human. People with the capacity to hate or fear have been directly affected by what they come to know about us through someone in their lives, or someone of whom they have an acute awareness, such as a celebrity or a character they come across in a movie, a television show, or a book. And interestingly enough, a public figure or figment of fiction is often the first way that a lot of people—LGBTQ included—encounter a queer person.

But no matter how other people or society feels about someone's shift in sexual identity, what matters most is how you see yourself. In this book are fantastic first-person narratives that detail what it was like for women who didn't always know they were bisexual or queer or lesbian, or even that they had the capacity to fall for another woman—regardless of what label they would take on or reject completely. But besides the new label (or lack thereof), there are so many other things to take into consideration. Aussie Ruth Davies shines a light on the lack of equality she still faces in her country. Pat Crow details life as a newly minted baby dyke on the cusp of sixty in "Straightening Myself Out." Vanessa Shanti Fernando discusses how she found the confidence to stop trying to find herself in lovers and see that she, herself, is enough. And Jeanette LeBlanc writes, "I was gay and I loved him and both things were equally and impossibly true," a sentence so heartbreaking and hopeful at once, that defines how contradictory self-discovery can be.

Just like *Dear John, I Love Jane*, this book is an offering of true stories that shows that whenever you find another piece of what you are, you can more fully become *who* you are. And if that piece is based in and inspired by something as universally desired as love, there is less and less room for criticism, and more for respect and understanding.

A woman who finds herself to be gay later in her lifetime is lucky to have found herself. We're all lucky to find ourselves at all.

Introduction I

BY CANDACE WALSH

I WRITE THIS INTRODUCTION SITTING ON THE COUCH IN the house Laura and I have shared for five years as a married couple. We produced *Dear John, I Love Jane: Women Write about Leaving Men for Women* when we were still just girlfriends, madly in love, but living in two different cities, aiming to make our two lives into a shared one but still figuring out exactly how to do it. Things have changed since then. The world has changed, too.

When *Greetings from Janeland* hits bookstore shelves, seven years will have passed since the publication of *Dear John, I Love Jane,* a groundbreaking exploration of sexual fluidity through intimate, firsthand stories. It remains a crucial resource for women who find themselves floundering in the knowledge that although they have (mostly) identified as straight, they are now madly in love with another woman.

Why *Janeland*? As I conceptualized this book, I kept having a vision of a shared land that came into existence because of the first book. *Janeland* is occupied by the essayists, of course, and everyone who read or will read the first book. It is occupied by all the women who have lived the book's premise. It's very inclusive—it understands the fluidity of sexuality, and offers shelter to women who have previously identified as straight, who consider themselves to be in love with women but not gay, as well as to women who identify as gay, bi, poly, or queer—that is, if they don't eschew labels.

In the first book, one writer maintained an open marriage with her husband and had a girlfriend. One woman wrote an essay about how she left men for women, but years after the book was published, as I write this, she's expecting a baby with her new husband. Desire is full of surprises. In concert with our society's greater ability to comprehend and accept that the gay/straight binary is as ridiculous as a slender crayon box with room for only two colors inside it, *Janeland* also holds space for unconventional versions of an already unconventional story line: girl meets boy, girl meets girl, boy loses girl, girl finds true love. One of our writers encountered *Dear John, I Love Jane* as a cloistered young wife who later fell in love with a trans woman, came out, and transitioned to a non-binary gender. Another woman left one heterosexual marriage in search of love with another woman, but surprised herself by marrying a man who not only satisfies her soul's needs, but understands that she needs to have the freedom to have a girlfriend, too.

And there are the many, many stories in *Janeland* that throb with the incandescent power of brave emotional truth.

When I pitched this book to Cleis Press, I didn't know that the deadline for this book would coincide with the day the electoral college would be voting for the next president of the United States. And I didn't know that those votes would not be for the woman I believed would be carried into the White House on the tide of progress that had granted same-sex couples marriage equality in the U.S.

To be fair, there were signs that our path would not be a breezy, linear one. North Carolina's HB2 law, commonly referred to as the "bathroom bill," which prevents local governments from expanding anti-discrimination and employment policies; threats to reverse marriage equality; and the brutal massacre at Pulse, a gay night club in Orlando, Florida, that killed or injured over one hundred people preceded the night Hillary Clinton's Javits Center celebration turned into a shocked wake.

In the tearstained blur that followed Election Day, I turned to editing essay submissions for *Janeland* and felt the first stirrings of strength and hope, an inner surge of pushback, that reminded me that I (and each of us) have the power to change minds, shake up the status quo, and dissolve hatred by telling our stories.

That may sound very ambitious, but the dozens of women who wrote to me after reading *Dear John, I Love Jane* are the ones who proved it. Before *Dear John, I Love Jane*, several of the women who reached out said they had felt devastatingly alone, even saying they felt "freakish." After finding the book, readers have been passionately grateful; many have told me that the book saved their life. Emboldened by reading stories like their own, these women started finding each other online and formed private Facebook groups to connect—I've even noticed people using the word "Janes" to refer to women who left men for women.

After Election Day, I felt fortunate that I could do more than sign petitions, tweet, and share articles. I was in fact, legally contracted to deliver a manuscript with 80,000 words worth of truth bombs.

Anxious women—who have little or no framework for understanding or acting on their radical, disruptive feelings of love—have a tendency to Google. And this searching, which accompanies inner searching, and tossing and turning, and guilty feelings, and dizzying imaginings, has led thousands to *Dear John, I Love Jane*. Now it will lead them to even more stories like their own in *Janeland*, too.

Introduction II

BY BARBARA STRAUS LODGE

They packed their cars and left the next week.
Yes they did, just like that.
Then there I was, whoever that was. Sliced wide open
and left for dead. While Verena was in Utah holding
[her ex-girlfriend's] hand looking at the red rocks, I
was in the wake of the storm holding a mirror looking
at a stranger. The woman I saw was tired and scared,
yet remarkably athletic for her age. I couldn't take my
eyes off of her and wanted to know more.
That's where the story really begins . . .

Leigh Stuart, "Mirror Image,"
Dear John, I Love Jane

I WROTE "MIRROR IMAGE" UNDER A PEN NAME, LEIGH STUART,
still reeling from all that had come before and ever so grateful to be
contributing my piece to such an important book. While my essay
about being married to a man and falling in love with a woman
didn't end wrapped in a happily-ever-after, lovingly coupled red
bow, writing the truth of my experience gave me strength.

After my "catalyst" (the beautiful, dreadlocked German
lesbian with emerald-green eyes who shook me from my marital
stupor) left me, I learned that my husband of fifteen years had
been cheating as well. His object of desire? Bags upon bags of
cocaine. After divorcing him, I embarked upon a year of field

research to determine whether I was interested in dating men or women. I didn't trust my instincts and needed to slow down, explore and observe. The scientific method I used was dancing in lesbian nightclubs with a group of new friends vs. dating a man every now and then. My experiments yielded an unsurprising result. I was undeniably drawn to women. Soft, communicative, strong, brave, outside-the-box women. Good with children and pets. Self-reflective and secure in their sexuality.

And as the story goes, I ultimately reconnected with someone I'd known in high school. She'd been a star basketball player back then, and while we were not friends, I recalled us giving each other the tall girl nod when we passed in the halls. She went on to play in college and still, almost forty years later, plays basketball with the men at her local YMCA. She is a Reiki Master Practitioner and, as we like to say, is the steady tortoise to my hurried hare. She's kind and rooted in the present like a wise oak. This woman brings out the best in me, and, above all, we travel the road of self-discovery side by side, learning and sharing our individual journeys. We are remarkably athletic for our ages. Every single day, even after eight years together, I awaken wanting to know more about her, and us.

When Candace invited me to co-edit *Janeland*, I didn't hesitate for one minute. I knew how vital *Dear John, I Love Jane* was to myself and other women, and I believed that an updated version would bring such stories to the forefront once again. Candace calls the essays in this book "truth bombs," and I couldn't agree more. Whereas I was once "left for dead" from the explosion that was my life, reading about the courage of other women inspired me to gather up a truer version of myself and forge ahead. There is a certain grace inherent in "meeting" those who've also experienced such awful, wonderful awakenings. The incredible essays in *Janeland* serve as continuing assurances that we, in all of our complexities, are not alone.

Sir, May I Have a Pack of Marlboros?

BY BK LOREN

I'M STANDING IN THE THRESHOLD WEARING A TANK TOP and torn boxers, my hands gripping the top of the doorway. I arch my body forward like a bow and arrow when I talk. "I don't even like women," I tell her. "They bug me. Even when I was a kid, I never really liked girls." My body is lean and muscled, the elastic of my boxers stretching like a bridge across the gap between my hip bones. "I'm not a lesbian!"

She is some kind of beauty queen—that kind of lilting loveliness that makes people look on from afar, afraid to get too close. I've seen childhood photos of her wearing a lacy dress, baby-doll shoes, a delicate way about her that I never had as a kid. I was always muddy, skinned up, bruised. My childhood photos are an embarrassing mix of me in only white underwear or, occasionally, wearing chaps and holsters over those white undies, a toy gun swinging from my side. I was rarely fully dressed, and I never brushed my long blonde hair.

But Sawnie, she has delicate features and smooth dark hair. Her eyes have this way about them. They are dark, quiet, confident.

The man I've lived with for the past several years, the man I'm going to marry, calls her "Beautiful Sawnie." Never just Sawnie. He lets me know that if he could, he'd be with her. But he is short, and she is tall, and to him, that's the end of the equation.

My equation is a little less clear. As I state my disavowal of women to Sawnie, we've just gotten out of bed. Together. We were not sleeping. I watch her dress, and she looks at me in this elegant way, a side-glance of disbelief. "Listen to yourself," she says quietly. She brushes past me in the doorway as she leaves the room.

A few days later, I'm with David. We walk into the bedroom, and there's a broken wine glass on our bed. Under the shards stained with red is a book by Adrienne Rich. The title refracts through the glass: *A Wild Patience Has Taken Me This Far.*

Sawnie has been here, in this house, in this room.

When I was a kid, I was a martial artist. Because Chinese martial arts were rare in the US at that time, I was the only girl in most classes. I fought against men. More often than not, I won. When I was done sparring, I heard people whisper, "Wow, what a dyke." I was twelve. I didn't know what the word meant. I thought they were calling me a dick.

Before the day I declared my dislike of women, David, Sawnie, and I shared the kind of friendship you can only have in college. You live together, become a family. You stay up until midnight becomes dawn, talking about all the ways you'll shake up the known world, make it a better place. You philosophize, dream.

The three of us had that kind of friendship: intense, intellectual, intimate. Sawnie and I also had the quintessential girl-to-girl friendship that blooms in college. We talked about the boys Sawnie dated and about my relationship with David.

Then came the tectonic shift.

It was winter, snowing now for the third day in a row. There's a particular beauty to the way snow falls on the front range of the Rockies in Boulder. The reddish-brown rock slabs that we call the Flatirons catch snow in their crevices, like lace draped on a dark background, the delicacy of early winter. David was out of town for holiday break, and at nine a.m., I was lying in bed, looking out at the Flatirons, ensconced in quiet. I curled up, pulled the blankets under my chin. I was swaddled in that sweet, liminal space between dreaming and waking, and Sawnie knocked on my door. My eyes opened halfway. "Yeah," I said, "come in," and she opened the door, stood there, her fingers and hands close to her mouth, fidgeting.

"Wanna go to breakfast?" she said.

I clicked my teeth, shook my head, no. "Too cozy in bed, Sawn." I pulled the blankets tighter.

She remained in the doorway, fingers still fidgeting. "I have to tell you something."

"So tell me now."

She shook her head. "Not in the house. No way. Not in *this* house."

Not in the house? What the hell did that mean? She said it with exaggerated conviction. It was part of her odd preoccupation—a recent change in her. Still, she had me hooked. What words could possibly have been so impossible to utter *in this house,* especially on a snowy morning when neither one of us had a reason to step outside?

When we did step outside, I really began to question her. Slanted snow slapped my cheeks. Everything stung. The ice of the week's storm sat in black mounds on the roads and sidewalks, fresh snow dusting it. It was so slick that Sawnie and I had to clutch each other's arms and waddle so we didn't fall.

"Well, this is fun," I told her.

"Oh come on. You're tough. It's nothing." She suggested

I keep my mind on the hot coffee and cheese omelets awaiting us at the College Cafe. "It's cozy there, too," she said. She was wearing this long wool coat that made her seem simultaneously more sophisticated—like some highbrow artist from New York—and more scary. It fell around her shoulders like a black cape. In the weeks leading up to this day, she had been critical, distant, sometimes mean, one of the first fractures in our friendship. I had begun to think of her as utter darkness, something shadowy and nondescript.

We walked under amber streetlamps haloed with snow. The sun struggled through haze. It took us about thirty minutes to walk less than a mile, and during that time, something happened. We began to laugh, to tell stories, to finish each other's sentences, like we used to. She said, "Remember that time in the UMC . . . "

" . . . when we crashed that display about Springsteen?"

She nodded. We'd spent many days pumping our working-class fists to Springsteen's lyrics, so when the Young Republicans put up a display at the UMC (Colorado University's student union) celebrating Springsteen's *Born in the USA* as a paean to war, we could barely stand it. So, late one night, when the UMC was virtually empty, we wrote Bruce lyrics on construction paper and plastered them over the misguided sentiments. When a janitor saw us, we ran like bandits out of the UMC, leapt over a wall, crouched low and huddled together, our hearts slamming our chests, our bodies close and afraid.

As we walked in the snow that cold morning, we laughed about our prank.

"Was there *really* a janitor chasing us?" I asked.

"I think so, yes," she said. We laughed ourselves to tears.

Just before we reached the greasy spoon, she turned to me, and the scowl of worry darkened her face again. "I'm scared," she said.

"Of what?" It was ten below zero, and I was losing my patience.

"I have to tell you something."

"So *tell* me. It's fine. Just tell me."

"Okay," she said, said it like she was steeling herself against some horrible news. She gritted her teeth and began to speak. Just then, I let go of the crook of her arm to open the door. The ice was slicker than we both imagined, and our feet skated to catch our balance. We laughed, and then Sawnie went down. Hard.

Still laughing, I stretched out my hand to offer her a lift up. She shook her head no, grimaced in pain.

Later that afternoon, I visited her in Boulder Community Hospital where she'd had surgery to put a steel shank on the broken bones in her leg. I brought her flowers, and I sat at the end of her bed, my hand resting on her cast. "Jesus Christ, Sawnie, I can't believe it."

"Yeah, pretty shitty," she said, and shrugged. "So, is David home yet?"

I looked at my watch. "Yeah, he should be home by now." I had brought her a stupid wind-up toy, a tiger that balanced on a ball, then flipped and landed upright again. I wound the key, let the tiger flip, then did it again. "So what were you going to tell me?" I asked. The tiger flipped, landed, flipped, landed. I wound the key tight over and over, waiting.

Eventually, she said, "David's home. You should leave now."

In high school, I was known for three things.

- My goal in life was to fake my way into a mental hospital. I believed I'd be happy there. In the outside world, I felt straight-jacketed.

- I was imperturbable. I'd learned this from years of study in martial arts. People would try to make me angry. They'd throw fake punches at me. I'd dodge and never show an emotion.

• I didn't like guys. That was my mantra. "I don't like guys." No one ever questioned me. Until one day, Bobby Rossi asked me out on a date, and I said, "No thanks. I don't like guys," and Bobby said, "Well then what *do* you like?" I thought of the possibilities. Birds. Mountains. Drawing. Martial arts. Quiet days on the ocean when I ditched school. Carole King. James Taylor. Janis Joplin. Other than that, I had no idea what the answer could possibly be.

Before winter break ended, David went out of town again. That afternoon, Sawnie clunked into my bedroom, full cast on her leg, and said, "I want to take you to dinner." Déjà vu. She fingered her mouth nervously, and she said she had something to tell me *outside of this house.*

The mystery had become a tick digging under my skin. I wanted to flick it off, but its tiny pincers had taken hold. So the three of us—me, Sawnie, and the massive white cast on Sawnie's left leg—clunked up the stairs of the Rio Grande Cafe. We had barely been given menus before Sawnie said, "I just want you to know, I don't want anything from you. I just need you to listen."

Ah, Jesus, really, here we go again with the drama. I struggled not to roll my eyes. I ordered a margarita. Sawnie drew in a huge breath, started to speak, and I took a huge gulp of tequila, because whatever she had been waiting weeks to tell me was finally on the tip of her tongue.

"Okay," she said. I leaned in. "You're not in love with David." I forced myself to maintain eye contact, sipped my margarita, puckered from the salt and lime, and she added, "You're in love with me."

My eyes went droopy. I was suddenly emotionally exhausted, and I think I muttered something to the effect of, *Oh, yes, this is very interesting; please do tell me your theory, because I do want to hear everything you have to say, and I have a very open mind, and I'm a progressive, forward-thinking liberal who has crawled my way out of a regressive, backward-thinking, redneck family, and so I want you to know that if you're a lesbian, I fully support you. And I can't wait to get home to David.*

She then methodically replayed all the times when I had "proven" this love to her. That time in the bar when the guys wouldn't leave us alone and I wanted them to think we were lovers, so—as defense against their advances—I leaned forward to kiss her. I stopped just short, when the guys began to holler out in disgust. That time in our home, when David was not there, and we were laughing, and we brushed shoulders, and our lips got a little too close. That time, those several times, when David was trying to talk to me, but I could not stop looking at her.

Halfway through her litany, a waiter passed, and I waived him down. "Sir, could I get a pack of cigarettes?"

"What kind?" he asked.

Up until this exact moment in my life, I did not smoke.

I envisioned the tough guy on the horse. I needed him now. "Marlboro," I said.

A few seconds later, the server was back. I opened the package, lit a cigarette, inhaled, and looked back at Sawnie with my completely open mind.

I was eighteen years old. Melissa was twenty-two. We shared an apartment together. I had helped Melissa through a relationship with a guy who had physically abused her. I was teaching her the self-defense aspects of martial arts. It was the 1970s. There were no safe houses for women in the state of Colorado. Melissa and I didn't have the money for an apartment with bedrooms. So we shoved two beds into a studio, made them look like an L-shaped sectional, and called it home. Then one night I was taking a chicken casserole out of the oven when I turned and ran smack dab into Melissa. I bobbled the casserole dish; she helped me steady it, and our arms and hands got tangled up. The casserole was the only thing keeping us from accidental full-frontal contact. We stood there, face to face. A few seconds passed. Then Melissa said, "Sometimes I think I could kiss you," and I said, "Would you like some chicken casserole?"

They say sucking cigarettes is sexual sublimation. I sublimated a whole pack of Marlboros as Sawnie talked. My throat felt like it had been scrubbed raw with steel wool. She talked. I smoked. I drank. I rested my chin on my twisted-up arms. I wanted to fall asleep. I was beyond exhausted. Two hours later, when she was finally done talking, my energy returned. "Okay. Ready? Let's go!" I said.

We walked down the stairs together, Sawnie leaning on one crutch and the bannister. "So, what do you want to do?" she asked.

Dinner was over. It seemed obvious. "I wanna go home."

"David'll be home tomorrow," she said, another obvious thing.

"Yeah. So, I'll pick him up."

"That's what you want?"

I shrugged. "Yes."

When we reached her car—one of those trashed-out, boat-like Buicks that parents handed down to their kids in the 1980s—I had to help her and her cast into the driver's seat. I took her crutches, leaned them against the back door, and she rested her hand on my shoulder for stability.

She rested her hand on my shoulder.

I was a martial artist precisely for this reason. The body needs defending. What touches the body makes an immediate impact on the soul. The body is fragile, the thing that holds the heart, the mind, the spirit. The body is the object of us, the thing that cannot be abstracted, the thing that cannot lie, the thing that finally broke down and made me give in to whatever I'd been fighting for years.

She rested her hand on my shoulder.

I was a kid again. I felt my body sweating, training, sparring, winning, and I heard the whispers, *she's a dyke, a dyke, a dyke,* and I didn't want to be *that,* whatever it was. I wanted to fight against it, the thing that diminished my power, that took away the fact that I had won, over and over, fair and square. I had won, and it did not matter, because I was a dyke. I felt the social straightjacket of high school, *Then what* do *you like,* and my utter silence that followed, and I watched my heart become something I could not fathom, could not see, name, hold, could not love.

She rested her hand on my shoulder.

There was the possibility of love. There was the possibility that I did not have to fight, that I could be me, whatever the fuck that was, because it had been lost beneath two decades of—what? Not lies. Not deception. Not denial, because I would've had to have been able to name the thing to deny it. I didn't even have a word for the unnamable mechanism that had kept me from naming the unnamable thing that was smothering me.

She rested her hand on my shoulder. She saw my body soften, maybe for the first time ever. She said, "My parents have a cabin in Estes Park. We can go there if you like."

My voice was shaking. I said, "Drive."

I called David the next day, told him I was spending the weekend with Sawnie in the mountains.

"Beautiful Sawnie?" he said.

"Yes, beautiful Sawnie."

I came back a few days later with bits of Sawnie's cast embedded in my face, my hands, my legs, my body. I came back with the thing that was healing her bones embedded in my skin. I hoped those specks might sink into my bones, do some kind of healing of my own, something deeper than I could fathom. I came back, and I said, David, I'm sorry. I didn't know. *I did not even know there was an option.*

Because there wasn't.

That weekend, Sawnie and I read Adrienne Rich's *Compulsory Heterosexuality.* It explained why the word *dyke* scared me. It peeled back layers of culture, violence, and oppression, and revealed a whole new color wheel of possibilities, of truths, of ways to live my life with integrity. I'd spent my college days studying Greek, Latin, physics—anything that might prove a recovering redneck like me belonged in a university. Sawnie spent her college career learning about the various forms of oppression in our culture—one of the oppressions that we, right then, were both coming face-to-face with for the first time.

When we were up at the cabin, she also showed me a story she had written. We both hoped to become writers someday. It was a vaguely fictionalized version of our lives over the past few months. In it, the main character's mother asked her why she had chosen to be with women. The main character's reply? "The only choice I'm making is whether or not to live an honest life."

There is a question of choice going around these days, the hot topic that allows others to define my life. Let me simplify it: Who I love is not a matter of politics or biology. It's a matter of the human heart. I do not have any more choice over who I love than you do. As Andrew Solomon has said, "We don't allow freedom of religion because Jews can't help being Jewish; we grant it because we believe in the value of self-determination."

The relationship I shared with Sawnie never really ironed itself out. But we had both crossed a threshold together, an unbreakable bond, even across time, distance, and silence. We moved on from one another, dated other women.

It's thirty-five years later as I write this. I've been with the love of my life for almost thirty years. And because love is a fluid thing that blooms in different ways at different times in different people, Sawnie has been with the love of her life for decades, too: an artist, an outdoorsman, a good man I know and care for.

Sometime last month, Sawnie and I talked comfortably for the first time in decades. We didn't pump our fists to Bruce Springsteen, but the bond we once had was still there. Because, yes, we had, in our own ways, shaken up the known world. Or at least, we'd shaken up our "known" world. We had made a difference. We had made the choice to live honestly.

Thirty years later, I finally understand that woman standing in the doorway in the "wife-beater" tank top, arching her body like a weapon and declaring to Sawnie that "I don't even like women. I'm not a lesbian." I understand, because I'm still her, with that kernel of self-hatred lodged in my bones, the anger that rises, the frustration that still, sometimes, blocks me from who I am. Because, in some way, we are all that woman. We live in a world that, like me three decades ago, hates women and does not even know why.

We, I, am also no longer that woman. Because one night, Sawnie had the guts to say what she felt, and because I finally had the courage to step out of the ring and into a fight worth fighting, one that would, eventually, give me peace.

A wild patience had truly taken me that far. In the book of poems refracted through broken glass on my bed so long ago, Adrienne Rich wrote of romanticizing language, of its power for disguise and mystification—the way words can "[translate] violence into patterns so powerful and pure we continually fail to ask are they true for us."

What is true for me:

I wake in the mornings, and I see Lisa sleeping next to me, and I know I am home. This is not a privilege granted to me with ease.

This is a hard-won right that has come to me over time, something I know more than I know even my own collective history, my own roots, which in the past, had become—even to me—a lie. Don't ask me to lie anymore. This is what I know. This is where I come from. This is where I belong.

Lisa and I walk our dogs in the saffron light of dawn. We plant tulips in autumn and watch them bloom in spring. The cycle repeats, and it is never repetitive. This love renews. This love stays. This love is not yours to name.

There is nothing I know more than this.

The Hemingway

BY ADA SCOTT

I WAS A JANE, THE COMIC-BOOK KIND. I WAS THAT WOMAN
who clung to the man who clung to the vine. I kept my strongest
opinions to myself. I took care of our child. I put my ambitions on
hold. I allowed my husband his Tarzan position. And I pretended
I liked it. When I was home cooking dinner. When I was sitting in
the park with other mothers, watching my daughter run around
the monkey bars and swings. When I was between the sheets.
I'd always looked at other women, found them more beautiful
than men, found their lines more appealing, but I didn't move
my thoughts to the place of fantasy, and, when I eventually did,
I never moved my fantasies to the place of reality, not for a long,
probably too-long, time.

Some thumbnail background may explain some things, not in
an easy, pop-psychology A equals B way, but in why I waited. I
was raised Catholic. I was one of three children, the youngest and
only daughter in a family where my dad worked construction and

my mom was, well, my mom. I was a rebellious kid, but my rebellion went to the smoking and drinking and sometimes drugging place. I made out with boys, not because I lusted after them but because that's what high-school girls did and because I liked the company of boys more than girls. Girls backstabbed and gossiped and talked about boys incessantly. Sure, boys talked about girls, but not so much around me. I got a kick out of the boys I hung out with, kids with small-town dreams and grease under their fingernails from auto shop. I enjoyed their rough language and their rough play.

I also felt protected by boys. To put it bluntly, my dad was a shit who hit my mom, my brothers, and sometimes me, and hated both his work and home life. He was basically a stranger who came home to eat dinner after work so his stomach would be full enough to drink heavy late into the night with friends. My most vivid childhood memory, one solidified by repetition, is packing a bologna sandwich for school lunch while my Dad snored on the kitchen floor. Scared to wake him, I'd step over his thick gut or between his sprawled legs to get the bread from the cupboard, the bologna and mustard from the fridge. School, not the academic side but the hanging-out side, became my refuge, and my small-town America school (especially as I moved through junior high and into high school) was about dating boys. I married the summer I graduated high school. Did I love the man? I loved some of him. He was kind, at least at first. Did I lust after the man? Sometimes. Did I want out of my home for good? Absolutely.

Fast forward seven years. I'm at the playground, watching my child dig holes in the sandbox. A woman sits down two benches away. I haven't seen her in this park before. She doesn't look like she's from around here. We look at each other, smile. She gets up and walks to a nearby tree and smokes a cigarette. I watch my kid play. I watch her kid play—he's a cute boy with the same curious brown eyes as his mother. She comes back.

"They need to make one of these for adults," she says. "A playground for adults."

"If only," I say.

"If only we could be adults and play without adult supervision."

I don't have a comeback right away. This isn't the usual polite back-and-forth between young mothers—no mention of the weather, no mention of how cute our kids looked—but I want to say something that would keep our conversation going. I want to find out what else this woman has to say, this woman with curious eyes, long brown hair pulled back over a beautifully symmetrical face, and a serene mouth that makes her words, full of daring, even more surprising.

"It's a nice idea," I finally say. "Without adult supervision. But think of the chaos. Without adult supervision even adults get in trouble. It probably wouldn't turn out too well."

"Maybe it would," she says.

That was Claire, starting the first of many of her sentences with *Maybe* to challenge my more conservative take on things. As we talked that morning and the next and the next, we became close. I couldn't wait to take my daughter to the park at ten every morning. Meeting Claire was the highlight of my day. Meeting Claire was the only thing I thought about, even as I made dinner or cleaned the house or weeded our small garden. And I thought about her body, moving from her forehead to her eyes to her lips to her neck and down.

Claire's history was very different from my own. She was a single mom. She'd just moved to our small town from Greenwich Village in New York City. She'd been auditioning there for a while, was in the acting unions, but the parts weren't coming to her, not the parts she wanted. When the pain of doing extra work in movies outweighed the joy of rehearsing for off-off Broadway shows that never advanced her career, she decided to quit. Her parents, New

Yorkers who had moved south for retirement, wanted to be close to their only grandchild and had set Claire up in a nearby house with a yard. Claire said she was getting too old for the parts she wanted to play anyway. I didn't think there was anything old about Claire. She was the best kind of beautiful, the most interesting kind of beautiful, breathless even when she was tired, when the circles under her eyes made me want to touch them.

One morning Claire came to the park alone. Her parents had taken her son to Disney World for the week. Claire said she wouldn't have been able to stomach the trip, the greed of the place, expensive tickets, long lines, failed actors dressed up as Mickey and Minnie, and all those snot-nosed kids begging for one more ride. I'd been to Disney with my child once. My husband had enjoyed it. I hadn't. When we took a day to visit Epcot Center, the fake Eiffel Tower in "France" and the phony canals in "Italy" depressed me.

Claire wanted to know if we could maybe (there was that word again but with an intonation I hadn't heard before) go out one night, to a bar instead of a playground. I got that sinking feeling, a roller-coaster drop different from the rides in Orlando. It felt familiar. I knew what it was, but I wasn't sure from when.

My husband had so many boys' nights out, he couldn't refuse me a girls' night.

Maybe, and I'm using Claire's word because Claire and I have been together for five years now, it's a cliché, but we went out on a Wednesday and something that had always felt a little off, a little jagged, a small chip on the lip of a familiar glass, went away. That night we drank, we talked, we laughed. We went back to her empty house—so different from mine with art on the walls and furniture that looked sleek and a kitchen full of spices I'd never heard of—and we sat on her sleek couch, two glasses of red wine on her sleek coffee table, and then she moved closer and sleek became warm became warmer and we did what adults do without adult supervision. This was different. But again it was familiar, something about it. I knew what a woman's skin would feel like. I knew what a woman's mouth would taste like. I knew what a woman's touch would feel like. And it wasn't because I touched myself, more lately, more than my husband lately. It was because I had fantasized more than I'd known for many years, more than I'd admitted, and my fantasies had been about women. Now my fantasies about Claire had become reality. I loved making love with her. I loved talking with her. The roller-coaster drop didn't stop. And I found myself. Or I found myself with her. I was the aggressor. She had started things, but I became the forward-moving one, which felt right, which felt me, making her cling to me, making her come first, then again and again. When we spoke afterward, when our bodies felt spent and we were resting, her head on my chest, the timbre of my voice was different, lower, comforting. I wanted to take care of her. Not like I took care of my husband in letting him take care of me. Not like I took care of my daughter. I wanted to take care of her, protect her, keep her beautifully serene mouth serene, remove some of the harsh dare in her words. And she wanted me, the new parts and the old parts under the new.

Claire was a reader. She started turning me on to books, real books, not comic books with one-dimensional Janes. What surprised me was that most of the authors Claire loved were men. She especially loved Hemingway. I'd read *The Old Man and the Sea* in high school, but didn't remember much. I remembered there was a shark that ruined everything for the old man. I remembered our teacher saying Hemingway didn't like women, didn't treat them well. I asked Claire about that. She said maybe Hemingway got a bad rap when it came to women. She said maybe if my English teacher had read more Hemingway and read him more closely he wouldn't have relied on what *they* said because *they* didn't exist and *they* were idiots anyway. Maybe Hemingway didn't treat women well in real life, but in his books, she said, he treated them as equals and better than equals because Hemingway's women were usually more interesting than his men.

Interesting wasn't an adjective I'd considered for men, not really. They were handsome or strong or stable or ambitious. Interesting was a rare color on the male spectrum that, blinded by the life I'd grown up in and by the life I'd led, I'd never noticed.

I thought about my husband. Was he interesting? Did he enlighten me? Did he make me see life differently or make me think ideas I'd never thought? Did he entertain me with his humor or some idiosyncrasy that made me smile? Had he surprised me in the last month? The last year? Ever?

In less than six months, after several girls' nights where we spoke more and more about a possible future, our dreams solidified. The what-ifs became concrete plans. I would move in with Claire. I would get a job, something I'd wanted to do for a while. And if the scandal became too much, if the stares turned to more than stares in our small town, we'd pack up our things and move one or two towns over. Her parents would be fine with that. Claire would sell her house and we could start anew together. All I had to do was break the news to my husband.

"That should be easy," I said, sarcastic.

"Maybe it will be," Claire said.

Maybe not. When I told him, he went through most of the five stages of grief in about five minutes. Shock turned to denial turned to anger, and the anger didn't abate. I flashed to my dad with my mom, his hand not just raised but lashing forward. Then I flashed to Claire and held my resolve. Finally, my husband's accusations turned to that most basic question, *Why?*

"It isn't fun anymore," I said.

If that sounded like a line, it was. It was Hemingway's lines and it was at the end of a story called *The End of Something,* which Claire had given me to read. The line was brutal in its simplicity, hurtful in its directness, but fit the moment so well: the lack of fun, the hum-drum of a routine that didn't ever include a Friday night dinner in a restaurant or a trip somewhere besides the single one we'd taken to Disney World or even a good-night kiss that might signify a kind of connection that wasn't totally taken for granted. My husband hadn't become my father—he didn't drink to the point of passing out on the kitchen floor, he never hit me—but if I had to write the story of our life together, there would be no climactic moments, nothing exciting, nothing fun. Hemingway would never have written our story, not if what Claire said was true. I, the woman in the relationship, wasn't the most interesting character because I was a very minor character. The story was my husband's. His job. His friends. The pressures he was under. The slights he felt. I was just there to support, a foil to whatever he was doing, feeling, thinking, which, as the years of our seven-year marriage passed, diminished because he shared less and less.

So that's why I said what I said. *It isn't fun anymore.* I didn't want to hurt him. But I wanted him to know that I too needed something, that what he'd become—absent—made *him* the uninteresting one, the unexciting one, the not fun one, not *me*. This was the end of something. A marriage. A lie I'd been living, or at least a half-lie.

My husband threatened to take the kid, but I knew he wouldn't. He'd changed a dozen diapers, maybe. He'd cooked a dozen meals, if pouring a bowl of Cheerios counted, maybe. He'd spend an hour with our daughter, coloring or playing house, but he'd be distracted after the first five minutes, checking his phone, watching TV, and when the hour was done—and it was always an hour, almost to the minute, as if he'd been timing the sessions—he'd hand her off to me and do whatever he did. He complained about work, but I knew, as soon as his pickup pulled out of the driveway every morning, he was relieved to be gone.

So when he made his threats about custody, I didn't say anything. I just started packing. He yelled for a while. He didn't yell for a longer while. The funny thing was, my husband had asked *why,* but he hadn't asked *who.*

It was only when he heard me make the call to Claire, asking her to come and get me, that he asked the question I'd most been dreading. I told him the truth. I'd met a woman. I'd fallen in love.

If there's a PG sheen to what I've written, it's a conscious choice. Even Hemingway didn't write the f-bomb. But when my husband found out I was leaving him for a woman, he went from pissed to red-faced furious. He called me a dyke. He called me a cunt-eating whore. He called me rug-munching bitch. He said I was worthless, a nothing, a nobody. He came as close to hitting me as he'd ever come. His hand was raised and I waited, waited. Then he kicked the wall, grabbed his keys, slammed the door, got in his truck, and drove off.

His vulgar accusations didn't touch me, but calling me a nothing, a nobody, opened something I'd known for too long about the back-moving me, the me I'd become too easily, more easily year after disconnected year.

When Claire picked me up, I could hardly open the door. I felt too tired, slow-motion tired. She picked up the bags I'd packed— one bag for myself, clothes only, two bags for my daughter, one for clothes and one for toys—dropped them in the trunk, joked with my daughter as she put her in the car seat, then came to me and held me for a long time.

"Maybe it didn't go so well," I said.

"Maybe not. But from here it will."

"Maybe it won't," I said.

"Maybe it will," she said and smiled.

Fast-forward five years. Claire and I are still together. She still makes me laugh, never takes me for granted, and is always curious. We read and we talk. We raise our children together. My ex-husband ended up moving to another state. He found someone new and has a daughter with her. My daughter visits him once a year. My life feels more honest now, more alive, and, while I cringe at some of the word's connotations, more blessed.

Which brings me to this summer. Claire had a surprise for me. I grilled her but she wouldn't cave. She said it was literary. She said it was Hemingwayesque. Hemingway had become our word for inclusion, not exclusion. The proverbial *they* said Papa disliked women, but in his work, and his work is all we really knew, he admired them. Lady Brett in *The Sun Also Rises* is more than just a pretty face. Maria is more than just a doting sidekick in *For Whom the Bell Tolls*. Marjorie in *The End of Something* is more observant, maybe even wiser than Nick. When someone excluded someone else based on sex, when someone diminished someone else based on sex, when someone assumed something about someone else based on sex, we called that someone a Hemingway Hater. When someone did the opposite, when their eyes were gender blind, we called them a Hemingway. That was our code.

I figured our Hemingway surprise would be a trip to Hemingway's home in Key West, Florida. It was an open-minded island, after all, where stares wouldn't linger and where everyone was a Hemingway, or so I'd heard. But I was wrong about the itinerary. Claire had bought us tickets to Pamplona, Spain, and we'd be celebrating at the festival of San Fermin.

It was a frenzy of music and dancing and sangria and, every morning, the running of the bulls. One morning, still bleary-eyed from the night before, we went to the bullring and watched the runners at the end of their run, coming into the arena, the bulls and oxen close behind. The runners, all men, looked relieved and giddy, like they'd survived something horrible and now, safe, could tell their stories, embellish them even, because what they'd done, if they'd run close to the bulls, was challenge injury, even death.

It was the height of macho, but there was something more, something universal and life-affirming in the challenge they'd taken and the challenge they'd won. They'd struggled. They'd survived.

"That looks exhilarating," I told Claire from our safe arena seat. "They look like they've lived through something and are better for it."

"The tradition seems a little forced," she said. "But they do look exhilarated."

"I'm thinking about it," I said.

"Don't. Those are real bulls with real horns."

"Don't be a Hemingway Hater," I said.

"It has nothing to do with your sex."

"Maybe it does," I said.

She smiled at that.

That night I was in and out of sleep, in and out of deciding. I woke early, an hour before the shot rang out that signaled the day's running of the bulls.

"I'm running," I announced.

"You're sure?" Claire said.

"I am."

"The runners aren't written about so favorably in *The Sun Also Rises*, you know. It's the matadors who get the glory, the ones willing to risk their lives for a few moments and look beautiful doing it. The runners, they're amateurs."

"I'm an amateur then," I said.

"Is it because it isn't fun anymore?"

"It's still fun," I said.

We were still in bed. I moved to her, on her. I kissed her long and slow.

"But this would be all mine," I said. "Not about you. Not about my child or your child. Not about the stares we've taken together, the comments, not about the hate that's out there. It would be mine."

"And this would prove something to you?"

"I don't know."

"Maybe?"

"Maybe," I said.

"Okay then," she said. "Let's get you dressed."

Claire got up, pulled one of her red T-shirts from a drawer, ripped it, threaded a piece of red through the belt loops of my white pants, a makeshift belt, tied a piece of red around my neck, a makeshift kerchief.

"You look brave," she said.

"I don't feel brave."

"Maybe you do."

I was nervous.

I walked, solo, to where the runners gathered at the end of town by the pens where they kept the day's bulls. There was a crowd of men. And there was me. Most of the men looked at me critically—a lot of Hemingway Haters. I imagined my ex-husband seeing me here, imagined the sneer, the words of criticism, or, perhaps more truthful, no reaction at all, that dead-eyed look that said he didn't know me and didn't care. I saw Claire's eyes before she kissed me good-bye. She was excited for me. She said she'd be waiting in the arena where we'd sat the day before, keeping her fingers crossed.

"You ready?" It was a man dressed in white and red.

"You're American," I said.

"Not today. Today I'm Pamplonan."

"Today I'm a Hemingway," I said.

He smiled, kind. He was a Hemingway too.

He told me to run fast, to keep running no matter what, no matter how scared I felt. He told me the most dangerous time was when the bulls were separated from the oxen and started charging all over the place. Those were called Sueltos, lone bulls. If that happened, or if I slipped or got stuck in the crowd, he told me to do anything I could to get out of the bull's way. In those moments it was every man for himself, he said. Then he smiled.

"Every person for himself or herself," he said.

"That sounds a little clunky," I said and smiled back.

I thanked the man and he wished me luck.

The waiting was the hardest. And that made sense. That's how it had been before I told my husband I was leaving. I hadn't had the courage just to tell him. I'd waited for the *Who?* and then, forced, I'd said I was leaving him for a woman. I didn't tell him I still cared for him. I didn't tell him about some of the good memories I had of us. The first thing I told him was something harsh, *It isn't fun anymore,* and then I told him I was in love with a woman. I wasn't gentle at that moment. I wasn't kind. I wasn't supportive. It was about me. I was scared and hurt from all the waiting I'd done, which, when I finally delivered that harsh Hemingway line, I finally understood. The wait to tell the truth, and the weight to tell the truth, had been the longest wait because until I said the words I didn't know if I'd back down and wait and wait and wait forever. Now I was waiting on the cobblestoned streets of Pamplona, but it was my waiting, mine, and the only fear I had to face was my own fear. And it was about being a woman too, being a woman surrounded by all these men and running with them. I was running with the men as much as with the bulls.

Then the stick rocket exploded, the signal that the gates had opened and the bulls were free to charge, and I didn't think about anything. I ran and I heard. Heard men's shouts. Heard pounding steps on cobblestones. Heard my own heavy breathing most of all. Then the oxen were near me. Then the bulls. And the runners, so many runners. And then the bulls were gone. The jolt of fear subsided in an unexpected way. I cried one long, loud moan, a giving up of something. Then I smiled. And I stayed smiling as I ran the rest of the run, through Pamplona's old streets, into the bullring, as close to Claire as I could get.

I waved to her.

She waved back.

On Being a Queer Jewyorican

BY SHARA CONCEPCIÓN

I WAS STANDING IN THE DOORWAY OF TYLER DINING HALL for the very first time, and she was sitting at the back of the room, wearing a white headband. The wolf in my stomach howled and kneaded and nudged from inside. The fireflies in my head glowed and faded like a pulse. The cicada long-burrowed in my heart threatened to climb out of my mouth and profess to the world: That girl over there, I want her hair on my pillow. I want her breath in my ears. I want her curved like a half moon against the cradle of my body. But what my body knew, my mind wouldn't, couldn't accept. My line of sight receded, and the dining hall stretched out before me: rows of round table tops, the soft angles of unfamiliar faces catching yellow light.

"I think the line for food is over there," said Maribel, pointing left. She was a fellow community college transfer to the Ada Comstock program at Smith College, my first ally in that strange new world.

I followed Maribel's finger, jutting out like a gun, to the mob of students inching towards the wafting smell of barbeque sauce. We joined the back of the hungry mob in their march, our backs to the girl in the white headband, but I swore I could feel her energy, a current moving through the air—past tables, past chairs, past the clutching hands of strangers guiding forkfuls to their lips. *That girl looks lonely*, I thought as I piled rack after rack of barbecued ribs onto my plate. I decided it was my moral responsibility to keep the lonely girl company. At least, that was the excuse I made for myself.

"Let's sit at the back," I said to Maribel, motioning with my head, and she agreed. Dinner in-hand, I wove my wide hips through the maze of tables between us until I was across from the girl in the white headband. I smiled dumbly as she methodically forked the mountain of spinach on her plate.

"Hi," I said as I put my plate on the table, "I'm Shara," and I stuck my hand out. The girl in the white headband dropped her fork and looked up at us dumbstruck.

"Hi?" she said in an intonation that suggested it was more a question than a greeting. Then, gathering her wits, "I'm Alex," and she took my hand. More people joined us at the table, all friends of Alex, the girl in the white headband. I was a little overwhelmed by the gathering crowd, but played it cool—worked the group in that unabashed, loud-as-fuck New York way, waving my hands in the air like an orchestral conductor and spewing just about anything and everything that popped into my head. And then, I started on about the ribs:

"They have so many ribs here!" I said, wide-eyed. "I've never seen so many ribs! Aren't ribs super expensive? Like, I can understand chicken, but ribs? And they don't even control our portions. How can they afford that, it's fucking crazy! It's impossible to go hungry here! But I'm gonna go home and put this in my freezer, just in case." I put my hand on the bulbous Tupperware lid in front of me, its clear plastic body revealing packed-in mounds of sauce-smeared meat. "Shit," I said, "if my family were here, they'd be all up in there like vultures, like scavengers. My titi'd take the whole damn pan of ribs home." Alex watched the elaborate hand show in silence, looking at me like I'd grown two extra heads.

"I can't believe it," I said, as I felt my heart well up with gratitude about just how lucky I was to be sitting there, at how far I had come, rough edges and all. "This place is magical," I said. "It's a dream." I smiled and studied Alex's confused face. She looked like she was crouching inside herself, head slightly bowed, pale eyes glancing up the way a nervous animal watches another animal. And then the left corner of her mouth pulled back. First a half-smile. Then a loud, hiccup-y laugh—a laugh that settled my body into my chair. A laugh better than therapy.

I skipped across the manicured lawns that night, under the starry Northampton sky, past the brick-red library, the ivy-covered halls, and quaint houses. The returning fall breeze broke like a caress, gentle on my skin, and I forgot the harshness of winter, the bitter sting of New England cold. In my dorm room, I sat in front of my boyfriend's two-dimensional smiling face, glowing dead-center on my laptop screen—he was finishing up a post-doc in England—as I prattled on about the never-ending ribs, and the girl in the white headband, and how incredible everything was. I laid in bed that night, restless. I looked at the pillow next to my head and tried to imagine my boyfriend's face, but I couldn't summon it. I didn't want to. Instead, in the dark theater of my mind, I saw her hair. Then the way she looked up at me, like she was stuck behind the windows of her eyes, like she was looking out. I imagined her laughing. *A good laugh*, I thought, and finally, softly, sank into a dream.

I entered those ivy-covered buildings the next day, the wood-paneled classrooms, spiral notebook under my arm, feeling like an alien in a strange, idyllic world. The air was brisk with the coming cold, and the day was full of new lessons; my professors, many of whom went by their first names, asked us to write our names on papers to display on our desks, along with our "preferred pronouns"—an exercise I'd never done before. Some students wrote "she, her, hers;" some wrote "they, them, theirs;" some even wrote "ze, zir, zirs." I learned that people like me, whose gender identity matched social expectations of their assigned sex, had a name, *cisgender*, and that others identified in other ways. Truth is, I didn't quite get the pronoun thing at first, but as a self-described Jewyorican, I could understand, even then, the pain of not having language to describe and validate one's existence. I also understood the power of naming one's self regardless.

Walking through campus, studying the sights with my outsider's eyes, I learned that students at Smith walked straight-backed, with purpose. That is, unless they were lounging in the perpetually green grass, making out. And suddenly making me uncomfortable.

I was preoccupied with getting to see Alex again. It took all kinds of unconscious self-discipline to stop myself from drawing obnoxious little hearts encircling her name in the margins of my notebook. I still couldn't accept my feelings for what they were: an all-consuming, horrible, wonderful crush. I was always a little different from most other people I knew—a little queer, if you will. As a young teen, I tried to wear difference superficially, like a badge of honor; I cut my hair into a fauxhawk and wore clothes that made people either too afraid to look at me or too perplexed to look away: spiked collars, combat boots, bumblebee stockings, and black tutus. Metal bars and hoops jutted from my face, and I even openly admitted to liking women. But in truth, I never thought of dating one. There was a barrier between me and that truth—one that transcended time and space, built up long before the name Alex ever rolled off my tongue. Unlike many of the students at Smith, I had no trust, no heirlooms, no inheritance. What I had were collective memories, and much of what I have become has been shaped by them.

My mother was a broad and excitable Jewish woman from New Jersey with paper-white skin and wooly red hair; my father, a dark-haired Puerto Rican with a knack for writing poetry, tinkering with electronics, and chasing things that made him feel good. He and his family had lived through the seventies and eighties, when nearly all of buildings of the South Bronx, the place they still call home, were charred soulless. It was a cityscape reminiscent of Dante's *Inferno*, with blocks of building facades dappled by blacked-out windows like punched-in teeth. While the Bronx was burning up north, queer people down in the Village, some of whom were Bronx residents, were also living through collective trauma. After the Stonewall riots of 1969, when queer people rose up against laws that made their very existence illegal, the movement and its proponents had become invigorated with a new sense freedom and self-determination. It was a kind of golden age. An age of freedom.

My father reveled in that new-found freedom of life in the Village, which became a hub of creativity, community, and exploration, sexual and otherwise. But he was not spared the fate of so many others; he contracted HIV the year I was born.

Life under these circumstances was difficult; year after year, I watched my father's body shrivel on his bones like dried hide only to grow plump again. It was like a cruel loop, and we were caught in its current. My mother also fared poorly under the circumstances life had meted out and had a difficult time meeting her own needs, not to mention mine and my brother's. By the time I was thirteen, I was living on the street and in friends' houses. By sixteen, I had flunked most of my high-school classes and had even dabbled in the drugs that might have been responsible for my father's fate. It was impossible to know how the virus entered his body—if it was through drugs or sex with men—so, until I put him into the ground when I was twenty-four (the number of years he survived), his suffering became inextricably linked to both.

I recognized that I had inherited a city less volatile than the one my father was raised in, two decades' worth of racial progress, and skin much lighter than his. There was the possibility of survival, but it was going to require sacrifice. Being a queer Jewyorican was out of the question; to survive, I'd have to pretend to be normal. And so, I grew my hair in long and brown, mimicked bourgeois patterns of speech, and pulled the metal from my face. I gave myself one rule: every job I took and goal I set had to involve community service; every struggle I faced, I'd work to make better for others. At the same time, I'd put up barriers to protect myself from a world I knew to be ruthless and cruel. Despite the great weight of my mask, the false starts and roadblocks along the way, my strategy worked; my record of service gave me a sense of pride and accomplishment. It also helped me snag a scholarship to community college and, eventually, a full ride to Smith College.

That first evening on campus, when I saw Alex across the dining room, everything I'd worked for since my youth—the normal life I'd fought for—was threatened.

Night after night, I stayed up late thinking about the soft waves of Alex's hair; her broad shoulders; and the cute, awkward way that she walked—more military march than gait. I spent my evenings plotting things to say to her. Still, I wasn't quite sure what I wanted. Though I had always felt attracted to women, dating them was so far out of the question that I'd never even imagined it. There were no models for that sort of thing in the particular pocket of New York that I came from. To make matters worse, I had always felt a kind of phobia during the rare times I did spot lesbian couples. It was a churning of the gut—a kind of embodied confusion, a mix of desire and fear that made me look away or walk in the opposite direction. But I was out of New York City and in Northampton—a city known for having more lesbians per capita than any other. Suddenly, I had undisputable proof that being a lesbian wasn't necessarily going to hurt me.

I dove deep into the world I had denied myself. I downloaded and watched every lesbian movie I could find. I discovered Ani DiFranco and memorized her songs. I turned to Google and YouTube to get a handle on "lesbian culture." I held the knowledge in my body, keeping it to myself until I couldn't keep it in any longer.

I told my boyfriend first.

Though living in England, he was a native New Yorker, like me. We had met at party he was DJ-ing when he was in town visiting his brother. I approached him and was excited to find out he was an engineer, as I had recently become enamored with the beauty and simplicity of physics, a cornerstone of his field, and we talked about it the entire night. That conversation led to hours-long messaging and Skype sessions about our lives, interests, and dreams. And now, it had led to this.

Although the chemistry wasn't quite there, I was committed to chasing normalcy, not romance, and here was this wonderful man—smart, kind, accomplished, and interesting—who seemed to be devoted to me. I figured I would have been stupid, I thought, to let someone like him go. But no matter how much I tried to pretend, the love I felt for him was strictly platonic; when I looked at him, there was no stirring or soft beating of wings between my hips. Just a simple sense of comfort and the care one friend has for another. Soon, the difference between my feelings for him and for Alex became evident; I could longer ignore what was happening.

"I'm a lesbian," I said. And just like that, it was out there in the world. It was the only word I knew to describe what I felt. "I see," he said, in a detached, matter-of-fact way. "That makes sense, I guess."

"Are you upset?"

"I'm not mad at you," he reassured, "but it's going to take me a little while to process."

We said our goodnights, and I went to bed a little freer. It was out there. That big scary "L" word. I said it. I owned it. And god damn it, I was going to keep saying it!

The next night, I sat under the harsh fluorescent lights of the campus cafe and tapped my grandmother's number onto my cellphone screen.

"Ello," she said, in a sleep-heavy voice.

"Hi Grandma," I said.

"Estephanie?" Grandma asked, like she was still dreaming. I imagined her sitting up in her oversized *bata*, switching on the lamp at her bedside, and putting on her glasses.

"No, Grandma," I said, "It's Shara."

"O, *Chara*," Grandma chimed, "*¿Como estas, Chara?* How are you?"

"Oh, I'm fine," I said, teeth chattering. Grandma sniffed out my bullshit through the phone like she had a sixth sense for it.

"*¿Y tu novio?* And your boyfriend?" she asked. I looked at the students around me, typing furiously and death-glaring at their laptops. Were they listening? Would they care? I suddenly regretted coming to the cafe for the call, but my head was spinning sick with the worst possible future scenarios. I didn't have the bandwidth to lift my body and walk away. My mouth couldn't, wouldn't make the words I desperately wanted to make.

"He's fine," I said, but Grandma wouldn't let me off the hook. She asked more probing questions. The more I danced around it, the more she pressed. Finally, I took a deep breath and forced the truth out.

"Um . . . Grandma?" I whispered, and I laughed a nervous laugh.

"*Hm?*" she answered.

"I like . . . um . . . I . . . how do I say this?" I felt my chest tighten, like my rib cage was closing in to protect my heart. "I . . . "

"*¿Que te pasa, Chara?* Ju wha?"

"I um . . . I . . . I think . . . I'm a lesbian," I said.

"Ooo!" she said, and then she laughed. "Obama estalking abou tha. And Ricky Martin, *el tambien es asi.* Ricky Martin is like that too. No worry," she said, "I still loving ju. I always loving ju, no matear wha."

I cackled into the phone.

"Thank you, Grandma," I said, and I wiped the rogue tear running from my eye. Unfazed, the furious typists kept attacking their keyboards, and the world kept spinning on its axis.

The next morning, I asked Alex to take a walk with me. I watched her from the corner of my eye—her worried face staring straight ahead as she marched her little march. My heart was raging in its cage.

"I just wanted you to know," I said, smiling like a maniac, because my face wasn't versed on what to do in such situations, "that I've had a huge crush on you for a long time." I felt lighter as soon I said it. Alex, though, seemed to absorb the weight. Her mouth struggled to catch and swallow air.

"I'm straight," she managed.

"I know," I said, still smiling. "I just needed to tell you." And I knew it was true in the moment it was spoken.

We said our good-byes, and I walked toward the back of the campus, to where Paradise Pond cascaded over the spillway. Alone, I watched the water sheet down in streaked reams, and I felt the fiery tips of my nerves dim to a soft luminescence. The wind rattled the branches and caressed my hair. It nudged me forward, and onward I went with my injured heart broken, but open nonetheless.

There was never anything more between Alex and me beyond a few simple conversations and looks across space. Eventually, I made peace with the distance between us; like me, Alex was living her own life and choosing what wholeness might look like for her. I was creating myself too; after I confessed to Alex, I was adrift in possibility. The title "lesbian" became a kind of lifesaver for me, and I held tight to it; I went to lesbian bars and pressed my sweaty body against other lesbians. I came out to my friends and family. As long as you pick a side and stay there, one had quipped. Otherwise you're just a slut. I swore up and down that I'd never touch a man again, as if that was the price of the ticket, of community. Soon, I had a girlfriend and a comfortable, middle-class life. But there was something uneasy in me. Lesbians, it turned out, were people too, heir to the same sins and virtues as everyone else, and my attraction to men didn't just disappear because of my professed allegiance to "the team," even though I sometimes wished it would. Even though I sometimes said it had. Something was amiss.

Day in and day out, I thought about sexuality. I read about sexuality. I mulled over sexuality with friends. I even enrolled in a Gender and Cultural Studies master's program. The deeper I dug, the more fear I pulled up. I was afraid of being rejected by the lesbian community, mocked by friends and family, thought of as confused or slutty. I resolved to reject that fear.

Today, I answer to myself, no one else. I want who I want, and I love who I love, regardless of gender. My feelings for Alex challenged me to confront the parts of my identity I'd sacrificed to get where I was, to feel the ache of loss, but not be defined by it. Meeting Alex made me larger, freer, and more capable of loving myself and others beyond boundaries, beyond fear. For that, I feel only gratitude. I look outward now, at a future marked by possibility, waiting to be made. I look inward, and I see a brave soul who just might step up and make it.

Seeking My Whiptail Clan

BY EMILY WITHNALL

AFTER I CAME OUT, I BECAME FASCINATED BY WHIPTAIL lizards. Whiptails are native to northern New Mexico, but I never took much notice of them until I was divorced and learning how to take care of my two small daughters on my own. Whiptails lay a clutch of eggs every summer, hatching between one and five baby lizards at a time. Their rate of reproduction was not what most compelled me, however. As a newly out, self-identified lesbian, I was drawn to whiptails due to their nickname: "lesbian lizard."

Whiptails are all female; there are no males. Technically, whiptails reproduce asexually, but in reality things are more complicated. It is through the act of mounting and biting other females that a whiptail can activate the hormones required for ovulation and the laying of eggs. Not only can whiptails reproduce without males, but they can also detach their own tails as a way to trick predators. While its removed tail flops around, the whiptail makes a run for the nearest juniper bush.

I never saw a whiptail in my own backyard, but I watched

them scrabble on the lichen-crusted boulders many evenings at my friend Melissa's house. Wine glasses in hand, we sat on the back porch, blasting Brandi Carlile and watching the erratic movement of the little yellow lizards with black spots as the sun set. Sometimes our daughters would count how many of them were missing tails.

The rocks still warm from the hot day, combined with the red earth, the pinks and oranges of the sunset, the grey peeling bark of the piñon trees, the pungent scent of juniper, and the existence of the spotted lizards were enough to assure me that although I was a single, queer mom, arriving to the awareness of my sexuality a little late, I'd figure it out. The lizards had clearly evolved, and I was in the process.

The first time I kissed a woman I knew for certain that my awareness had finally caught up with my body. It's hard to explain why it took so long. I am from an open, liberal family. But I grew up in a small, Catholic, Hispanic town and it was par for the course for young girls to begin dating at thirteen. I submitted to the pressure. Or, more accurately, I wasn't even aware that the pressure existed. To paraphrase Adrienne Rich— another late bloomer—compulsory heterosexuality compels women to conform to prescribed roles: girlfriend, wife, nurturer, mother. I filled all these roles awkwardly, inhabiting them much like the tiny doll clothes my daughters tried to stuff our cats into. I squirmed and wriggled, uncomfortable but not fully aware of why. In coming out, I have worked to shed or re-imagine these roles. Despite marriage equality, I have not reclaimed "wife." But the most difficult, ongoing challenge I face is in reshaping "mother."

On a smoky day at the end of August, I walked my daughters to their new elementary school in Missoula, Montana. We had just moved from New Mexico, and although the forest fire haze was not new to us, everything else was—the lawns in every yard, the flower gardens, the deer wandering the streets and grazing on fruit trees and hedges. The schoolyard was like something out of a Hollywood movie. Proud mothers and fathers arrived on foot or bike to help their kids find their new teachers. The students lined up dutifully in front of their teachers in a half-sun formation, each ray a different grade and classroom. My youngest daughter's teacher walked her line, hugging each child and asking them about their summer. The other parents smiled and waved and navigated unwieldy strollers. There was a lot to take in, but in all that I saw, there was something I didn't see. I did not see any other parents alone. I did not see a family with two moms or two dads. Not only was I the sole single mom on the playground, but I guessed that I was the only queer mom, too.

In New Mexico I hadn't had to worry about being an outsider. My daughters were born in my small hometown, and many of my friends had known me when I was married and when I believed—unquestioningly—that I was straight. So when I came out, I retained the community I had and added a few older lesbian women to my expanding circle of friends. It didn't bother me that many of my friends had husbands and lived heteronormative lives. After all, I had lived as a straight woman for six years before my divorce and subsequent coming out. But here in Missoula, I wasn't sure what I'd encounter in the way of community.

I hugged my daughters, each lined up in front of their teachers, and watched as the classes began trickling into the building. After my daughters disappeared, I lingered, catching snatches of conversation exchanged between other parents—camping stories, in-law visit mishaps, and European travel sagas. On one end of the playground, near the fence, a group of moms clustered around a circle of strollers. I overheard snippets of conversation as I passed by: "Alexander is an old family name" and "That's such a neat tradition" and "My husband really wanted to name

Aiden after his grandfather, but his name was John, and I once dated a man with that name." The women wore tank tops, Lycra leggings, and running shoes. Their ponytails were smooth with golden highlights, their long shiny hair a contrast to my tousled pixie cut.

George, a new neighbor from down the block, asked me who lived in the other half of the duplex I'm renting.

"Two young guys," I said. "One's in law school and the other is younger, an undergrad."

He raised an eyebrow at me, smirking. "Some eye candy," he suggested, "or more?"

I laughed uncomfortably. I had told him weeks ago that I had a long-distance girlfriend. "Um," I said, "I'm not into men."

He glanced at my daughters and back at me. I'm never sure what to say in these moments. It was certainly not the first. I decided I was tired. Not interested in explaining. So when he asked, making sure he fully understood, "You don't date guys, like *ever*?" I simply said no.

Men seem to have the hardest time with my sexuality. They don't want to believe I'm not attracted to men. I was married, after all. I had boyfriends in high school. I have kids. Shortly after coming out in New Mexico, a coffee shop regular approached me as I tried to leave with my mocha.

"I always see you in here with your kids. It's so hard to be a mom. You're doing a good job," he said.

"Thanks." I tried to edge out the door.

"What does your husband do? How come I never see him around?"

"I'm divorced." I smiled, hoping he'd see it was fine, hoping he'd get out of the doorway. Behind me, the coffee shop offered a backward retreat. The Saltillo tile was cool and the hand-woven rugs and tapestries that decorated the walls made the place homey and inviting. But I'd be late to work.

"That's tough," he said, shaking his head. "You're doing it on your own? Wow. Well I'm sure some young man will snatch you up."

He sounded like my grandma. "I'm gay," I said flatly. Madly. I wanted him to get out of the doorway. And although I had told the truth, I regretted my words as soon as they emerged. I watched as his face ran the gamut of surprise, shock, disgust, and finally, rage.

"When I lived in San Francisco there were all these homos, these men that would lay with other men," he sputtered. "Disgusting."

I stared at him evenly, torn between expressing my own rage and giving him a natural history lesson on whiptail lizards.

"I hope you don't date those women who think they're men, the ones who wear leather and drive motorcycles." He scrunched up his face as he spat the words out.

"Butch women?" I offered. I was dismayed by the deeply problematic stereotyping but aware of where he was going with this. He nodded.

"Oh, I am super-attracted to butch women," I said. I pushed past him to make my escape as he boiled over behind me.

I don't encounter such direct homophobia in Missoula. As people here say, Missoula is thirty minutes from Montana—a liberal blue bubble in a very red state. But when I eventually met queer women, I found we didn't have a lot in common. After a year of living in Missoula, I received a scholarship for grad school from an LGBTQ foundation, and I attended the event hoping to meet potential friends. Although I experimented with wearing baggy men's clothes for a very brief period after I came out, I quickly reverted back to my more feminine style. Coming out was like coming home to myself, not changing myself. So I chose a pink dress with roses around the hem from my closet and tried to tame the cowlicks in my short hair. But when I arrived at the reception I felt like an imposter. I was the only one in the room with kids, the only one who hadn't come out in high school, and the only one who didn't have a gut-wrenching coming-out story. When it was my turn to be acknowledged I decided against sharing my personal story and stuck with thank-yous. I was truly grateful to be seen by the foundation as a deserving and legitimate member of the community, but as is so often the case, "coming out" as a mom in queer spaces can make it hard to feel I truly belong.

Likewise, I am out of place on the playground at my daughters' school. I am familiar with the world the other moms there inhabit, but that is not my life anymore and I have no desire to return to it. Though it is easier to connect to straight women by appealing to our mothering connection, I often find myself listening in on conversations about what their husbands do or don't do.

At one work party I attended, mothers shared stories about how they discussed sex with their kids. I'm not sure why I was surprised when they each revealed the brevity of these conversations, their focus on heterosexual relationships in which the purpose of sex is reproduction, and safety only as it relates to pregnancy. I supposed that if I were a whiptail lizard, I could offer my daughters the same dry facts about how reproduction works, but in that moment I was most struck by my invisibility. In my role as mother, I was presumed to be a part of heterosexual prescribed norms. Though I was tempted to suggest that sex is not limited to procreation, and that their kids might not identify as straight, I worried that such comments would come across as being passive-aggressive.

Being read as straight certainly comes with a privilege I do not take for granted. Despite the annoyance of other women occasionally thinking I'm hitting on their husbands if I speak to them,

I do not generally fear for my physical safety. I do not have to think about whether or not to stop in a small town to use the gas-station restroom. I don't have to worry about nasty remarks or incessant questions about what or who I am. The inherently privileged flip side of this, however, is that my children render me invisible. When I first moved to Missoula and mentioned my girlfriend to a queer woman I'd just met, she registered surprise—a not-uncommon reaction to my coming out.

"I noticed the rainbow stud in your ear," she said, "but when you mentioned your kids I didn't think you could be gay."

My triangle-shaped rainbow earring is the last remnant of my early coming-out days, seven years ago. In addition to my brief stint wearing oversized clothing, I also wore more rainbows— and I came out in every conversation I had. I felt an urgency to proclaim my identity to the world, a need to establish myself in all my newly discovered authenticity following my divorce. Although I no longer feel this urgency, I do get lonely sometimes and long for a community of people like me. I am envious of friends and acquaintances who talk about queer communities they have belonged to. I am particularly envious of women who live in big cities and are a part of a circle of queer parents. I have always lived in small towns though, and I attribute the fact that the bulk of my friends are straight to this fact, and to my role as mother. To be clear, I love my friends fiercely and wouldn't trade them for the world. They have supported me in all the various stages of my journey. Still, I sometimes yearn to be a part of a community in which I can be both queer and a mom without feeling I don't quite belong.

My fascination with whiptails has everything to do with my attempts to reconcile my identity as mother and queer woman. I recall the endless hours I spent online before I fully came out to myself and the confusion I felt when, in online forums, I came across lesbian-identified women referring to straight women as "breeders." In my turmoil, I wondered if I could be gay if I had brought children into the world. My discovery of whiptails many months later provided solace. Their existence, and the evidence of their evolution as a species, helped me to understand that my identities were not mutually exclusive.

Though I am happy to report that I have never encountered "breeder" comments in person, I am still trying to figure out what it means to be both queer and a mother. I have become adept at compartmentalizing, talking about my kids with heterosexual women and limiting mentions of my girlfriend. Likewise, with queer folk, I focus on my queer identity, mention my girlfriend freely, and keep kid talk to a minimum. I'm not proud of this, and in the past year, I have made more of an effort to push past awkward silences and talk freely about both of these identities. However, I'm still not where I want to be, and social norms in the small towns I've lived in aren't there yet, either. The path I'm on has skittered erratically, and sometimes, in moments of perceived danger, I have had to disguise myself. I can't wait for society to evolve, and I understand that it's up to me to claim my queer-mother identity in the spaces I enter. As Adrienne Rich wrote, "When a woman tells the truth she is creating the possibility of more truth around her." And as I speak my truth and continue to reimagine and reinvent the roles I inhabit, I'm keeping my eyes open for my small-town whiptail lizard clan.

The Dealer's Gift

BY LOUISE A. BLUM

IT'S BEEN THIRTY YEARS SINCE I LAST SLEPT WITH A MAN,
but I remember them all: the Palestinian in Germany with whom I
lost my virginity—his inky curls and his liquid eyes, the undeniable
pain of that first penetration, for which I was entirely unprepared.
I remember the Arabic words he taught me, alone in the dark, as
we learned each other's bodies in a tongue that was foreign to
us both. I remember biking through Ohio summer nights with
the slacker stargazer in college, shedding our clothes and sliding
into the lake with the ease of dolphins to swim beneath the stars.
I remember the bartender in Omaha, how there was nothing
attractive about him until he hit the dance floor, where his body
took on the sudden grace of a heron striking water, morphed into
a vehicle for song. I remember the organizer from Chicago, who'd
spent the seventies with the Farm Workers, immersed in produce
boycotts in a city so far removed from those California fields as
to be nearly irrelevant. With his dark hair and beard and deep,
long-suffering eyes, he resembled no one so much as Jesus. We'd
listen to Simon and Garfunkel and make love on the same couch

where I would later have sex with his roommate, the unemployed construction worker with the ponytail and way too much time on his hands. I remember eating falafel at a halal dive in Cleveland with the canvasser who'd remade himself through EST and had three other girlfriends. I remember the way his hair fell across his brow, how the skin crinkled around his eyes when he looked at me. I remember driving for hours through the midnight rain in his VW Rabbit, gazing at his profile in the darkness and thinking I would give up everything just to have him. I remember the legal-aid lawyer in Pittsburgh with the shy eyes and the slow smile, whose wheelchair provided the opportunity for creative variations on what was by now a familiar theme. And then there was the drug dealer in Atlanta. That one was a low point, one that lasted three years. It was like kicking an addiction, getting out of the habit of him. I had to move to Iowa to escape him.

All those experiences, all those men, they all have one thing in common: I can remember so many things about them, the way they spoke, the accents and the idioms, the particular tell of each one's movements. I remember the longing I felt for the ones I couldn't have, the emptiness I felt with the ones I could. But one thing I cannot recall is anything about their genitalia. Try as I might, I can't conjure up a single penis. Not a testicle. I run my memory along their bodies until I reach—a blank space, as if a selective amnesia had descended like the night to shield my view.

In those uncertain days of my early twenties, life was a thing that happened to me. Those encounters, those men, were incidental, products of the simple intersection between time and place. I was there, they were there; we went with the flow. My job as an organizer meant that I never stayed in one place too long. I slept on people's floors, moved where the Organization sent me. I shifted cities mid-campaign, committed new streets and faces to the ever-expanding geography of my experience. I was a vessel for change, but it was someone else's change. True, the goal was a revolution, but even at twenty-one I knew those chances were slim. A stoplight at a busy intersection in an inner-city neighborhood was a good day. An underfunded school stripped of asbestos was a great one. A hundred people at a sit-in was a rush like nothing else I'd ever experienced. My job was not to lead, but to move others to lead, not to instigate but to incite, to allure, to nag, to prod, to prompt: a kind of subtle balance between manipulation and empowerment. I existed to do this job: whether my needs were met, whether I ate or slept or made a friend or saw a film was irrelevant. Was, in fact, dangerous. To the cause, perhaps. To the Organization—certainly.

I knew what the dealer was: he was my avenue for escape, my extraction from the constant interchange of politics and personality, a chance to lose myself in myself. The dealer lived next door; the convenience was a major attraction. The minute his door closed behind me, I was somewhere else. I was nowhere anyone could find me. And it lasted until I saw the light again. There was a kind of magic to it, a Wonderland experience: he played no part in the other aspects of my life, he never met my family, he had no interest in my job. Politics to him were an abstraction, as irrelevant to his life as he was to mine.

I knew what the Organization was as well: a powerful, all-encompassing, arachnid mechanism for change. And being a part of that was an intoxication, a hallucinatory reenvisioning of the world we lived in. And the attraction of losing oneself to a cause: saints have known it. Monks. Nuns. The lure of the hair shirt, the submersion of the self in something greater than oneself. The role of the martyr is perhaps the ultimate form of egotism, nearly irresistible. A line of coke on a mirror.

But martyrs die young, and nuns disappear into their cloisters. A vow of silence wears thin. Both the dealer and the Organization were drugs in themselves: satisfying at first, then less and less so.

I developed a tolerance I had no desire to overcome. And I was useful to the Organization only so long as I knew my place within their apparatus.

I suspected this went for the dealer as well.

I crossed half the country to make my new life: a writer's life. I was a settler heading west toward undiscovered territory: the ultimate American myth. Places are undiscovered only to those who have never been there. But as the hills gradually flattened out around me, as the wind rustled through the grasses on the prairie—it was all new to me. To look up into that biblical sky, dark and unending, flooded with stars, flush with clouds. To be in the presence of all that weather, absolute and unabridged, afternoons turning on a dime with the sudden descent of a silence so ominous it was almost holy. Every leaf stilled, paralyzed with expectation. The instantaneous golding of the air, the sucking blackening collapse of a funnel of clouds: this was indeed a brave new world, alive with portent, shivering with the approach of that which is unknown.

The dealer pursued me, in that way that we suddenly desire the unattainable: with an abrupt and unsettling urgency. The sudden presence of him in my Iowa City apartment threw my life into sharp relief. The drugs had been good, the sex even better, but this brave new world I'd constructed for myself was best of all.

I said good-bye in a coffee shop on an appropriately bitter Iowa December night. He took my hands and held them in his own, warmed them with his breath. It was the kind of detail he'd been good at. The small comfort gestures—the cut flower; the rolled joint; the proffered mug of coffee, black. It felt so good to break it off, a clean, solid break, the kind that renders the bone twice as strong as it was before. He kissed my hands, and then, with a single phrase, he determined the course of the rest of my life. *If you don't want me,* he told me, softly, *then you must be a lesbian.* His breath on my palms chilled my skin. His reasoning was, to him, readily apparent: I'd have to be a lesbian not to want a guy as sensitive as him.

I left him there, sauntered out under the starlit sky. I tried to laugh it off, but the black Midwestern winter wind stole the sound from my throat before it could leave my lips. I walked home alone in the pale light of a distant constellation, fighting the chill that settled in my bones, his words seeding themselves deep within my brain, where they lingered like a curse. *Then you must be a lesbian.* Somewhere deep inside, I had the nagging desire to prove him wrong. But if I had learned anything from that relationship, it was that I would rather be single for the rest of my life than settle for less than I deserved.

I fell in love with being alone. I spent my celibacy dancing by myself in clubs, hiking alone through the red rock canyons of Utah, sleeping under the stars at the Lama Foundation outside Taos, New Mexico, riding my bike through the gentle rolling hills of Iowa, trekking through the Sonora Desert in 116-degree heat with nothing but a compass and a jug of water for company. I drove through the night in my pickup truck across a country that unrolled on either side of me like a promise—alone on the road, my windows open and my radio blasting, singing as loud as I wanted because there was no one there to hear. And at night, alone in my bed, I came to know my own body with my own hands, and there was nothing any of those men could have done that I couldn't do better. If the curse he'd left me with ever crept into the forefront of my brain, I shrugged it off. I thought I could live the rest of my life just like this: needing nothing from anyone except myself.

I'd been alone four years when I moved back east for a teaching gig in a nowhere town in a nowhere place in Pennsylvania, surrounded by a mountain range I hadn't even known existed. I thought I was just passing through.

I never left.

I could blame it on those mountains, which enticed me into their midst, then closed me in. I could say it was all that green in all those trees, after so many years in prairie and desert. I could claim it was the water that held me fast, the way the mist rose from the river on autumn mornings to roll thigh-high through the streets, thick and moist and bodiless, a lingering presence marked by absence, a memory that couldn't last. Or the winter light, piercing the spaces the fallen leaves had left.

But the truth is, it was Connie.

I fell in love with her over morning coffees at the diner, after-work beers at the bar, conversations that went on for hours, at every time of day or night. I fell in love with her laughter, her smile, her tendency toward argument, her passionate embrace of everything around her, and I'd be lying if I said I hadn't noticed her breasts. But when she tried to take the relationship further, I froze. The dealer's refrain ran through the back of my mind on a constant loop, like a migraine that wouldn't quit: *you must be a lesbian.* Connie says I told her I was straight, but in truth I have no idea what I might have actually said to explain myself; I could hardly hear anything through the static of the dealer's curse.

I moved to a cabin on an isolated mountain top so far out of town that grass grew down the center of the road. I thought I could live my life alone, that I would never tire of my own company. But she was persistent, and before too long she managed to drown out even the dealer's monotonous prediction of doom. The first time she unbuttoned her sweater and unzipped her jeans unleashed in me a seismic wilding. I dove into her body as I would a gorge, heedless of the consequences, and when the water slammed shut above my head, I wasn't entirely sure that I would ever surface again. But if this was what it was to drown, maybe that was all that I could ever hope for. Her body pooled before me, and there in all its curves and contours, both enticingly familiar and evocatively foreign, was a landscape I had never seen. And what I discovered there was the magnificence of agency.

What I discovered as a lesbian was the joy of making love to someone. There were no rules and no predetermined roles, and I discovered in myself a mastery I never thought I had. It was like finding in oneself a sudden talent for art. There were a hundred different ways to make her happy. It was as if a canvas had been put before me, and I had only to touch my brush to it to make it sing. If there was anything in my life that resembled this in any way, it was my brief time with the lawyer in the wheelchair, whose physical limitations had proven unexpectedly erotic. But this body—these sultry lips, this crooked smile, the breasts and waist and belly and hips—it took me over. It inspired in me a passion that superseded any that had come before. The authority of giving and the utter abandon of her response surpassed anything I'd ever known.

The agency in this new geography was not limited to sex; it extended to other parts of our lives as well. There was no path in this terrain, no steps to follow. It was a blind stumbling forward, feeling with our hands for whatever was to come.

And if at times I wonder what it would be to go back, to embrace again the sexuality that marked my first steps into adulthood, I think of those forgotten spaces, that disconnect between heart and genitalia, the dissociative nature of my memory. I think of my dealer, of what he gave and what he took away, and of how the space between a curse and a blessing is measured only by perspective and by choice. And then I envision Connie's body, in all its silken radiance, so familiar and yet so undiscovered. I think of how I know the pitch and beat of her: the folds of her labia, the swell of her clitoris, the texture of her hair, the variegated shades of her vulva. I think that there is no separation in our union between the emotional and the physical, that what I know is chiseled forever in my memory, and that a lifetime will never be enough to discover everything about her.

And I think that undiscovered territory can be a place we live in all our lives.

On the Track

BY KATE ARCHIBALD-CROSS

I STOOD QUIVERING ON THE LINE, BALANCING PRECARIOUSLY on my toe-stops, waiting for the whistle to blow so that I could launch myself forward. I knew that once I started skating, muscle memory would kick in, and for two short minutes everything would be clear. My world would feel familiar, predictable, and safe.

Odd, perhaps, that my place of comfort was skating at top speed around a concrete roller derby track, anticipating full body blows at any moment, while dekeing around other skaters and watching for my own teammates to knock people out of the way to clear a path for me. But the comfort, freedom, and bliss I felt playing roller derby was a welcome respite from the rest of my life, which had become a foreign land to me.

It made no sense at all that I was here, squeezed tightly into a pack of ten women, playing like my life depended on it, when really, what was happening off the track would seem more worthy of my attention. I had recently told my partner and closest friend of fourteen years, the father of my kids, that I was sure that our relationship was over.

In the past few months, I had assured my partner that I wasn't changing, nothing was different; now it was clear I was wrong. It wasn't that I was lying when I said those things to him—I honestly believed they were true. It's kind of my thing, being the stable, predictable, reliable one, in any situation, and while I had some inner turmoil, I was confident my staid self would plod on, comfortable in the life I had made for myself and my family.

It was an exhilarating time—our derby league was large for a small city, and we had been around for just under a year. But over that short time, our group of sixty-six women had become incredibly close, and we lapped each other up: at practice, over postpractice beers, on road trips to watch other teams play. Our discussion boards sizzled with ardent conversations. We were obsessed with this, at-the-time emerging sport, its uniquely colorful culture, and each other.

It's not as common now, but when I was playing, it was the norm to choose an alter ego, a "derby name." Often, people's names would be clever puns based on their real names or interests. Names were frequently mashups involving the full-contact nature of the sport and/or sexuality.

The sport also provided a forum to reclaim a ton of language around the female body. It was not uncommon to walk into a practice and hear drills yelled out like "ass to vag" or "paint her pelvis." This felt risqué and empowering at the same time. Many of us weren't used to using or hearing language like this, nor were we used to consistently putting our bodies so close to other people's, but it felt okay—even good—here with these women. And we were learning how to use our bodies to move other people around or stop them from getting past us. As someone who grew up terrified of walking alone at night, learning to use my body to stop someone else from doing something I didn't want them to do was huge, and as my body became stronger and stronger, my confidence soared.

Our league was *busy*; we were in parades, we went to weekend-long training camps, we did pub crawls to promote our games, we booked high-end off-skate training to increase our fitness, we had karaoke nights, we brought in guest skaters to teach us more, we traveled to tournaments. After being home with kids for almost ten years, the opportunities to get out of the house to train, learn, and do new things were exciting, and as president of our league, I genuinely felt it was my responsibility to be part of all league events. And it was a fun responsibility, compared to the responsibilities of home, managing finances, never-ending renovations, and, despite my general comfort and contentment in my relationship, my complete lack of libido.

I met her on the track, of course, the woman who would alter the course of my life forever. We were thrown together into this heady mix of people and were drawn to each other instantly. Two seemingly very different people—me, straight, quiet, reserved, left-leaning, and historically sedentary; her, lesbian, brash, centrist, and very athletic—who shared a mutual love of derby. We became very close friends, having coffee, texting regularly, and simply loving each other's company, both on our own and with the league. She became my go-to person, and I was hers; from questions about training strategies to raising kids, we talked all the time, about everything.

Slowly, slowly, slowly, as we talked about all the things we loved and wanted out of life, I started to wonder if I was, actually, happy enough at home. I cared deeply for my partner—we had a good time together, shared a ton of experiences and memories, and were amazing co-parents to our two young sons. But maybe something was missing. Things I'd swept under the carpet in the past began to seem like clear signs that something wasn't right. I started to imagine my life outside of that relationship, and that vision, rather than the terrifying leap it seemed when I began the thought experiment, felt like a sigh of relief as I played it out. I wanted my kids to grow up seeing their parents do things that brought them joy—and I began to wonder if I had enough joy in my own life to model that for them.

So, of course, I promptly shoved those feelings way, way down and decided not to address them. Although I was starting to have more-than-friendly feelings toward my friend, which corresponded to the awareness that my partner and I were living more like housemates than soul mates, I wasn't going to rock the boat.

I dealt with the anxiety by finding new and better ways to keep myself busy and out of the house. She and I were moving beyond simple, close female friendship and toying with something more, but both of us were in long-term, committed relationships, and we weren't willing or able to end our relationships with our respective spouses.

Through it all, we skated. We sweated through grueling practices, pushed ourselves further physically than we'd ever thought we could go, and reveled in the pain, the bruises, the breaks. With this renewed dedication came increased empowerment, camaraderie—and fun. From the very first month of our league's inception (when at least three people left practice with broken bones), we became adept at having each other's backs through injuries and other traumas. Our meal trees were incredible. We developed strategies to help each other with childcare, we helped each other move. . . . We knew that we could count on each other both on and off the track.

It was common for very close friendships to emerge within the league, but eventually, after what felt like years—but was really just a few months—of agony, we had to admit that our efforts to keep our friendship platonic were failing.

I knew that once I acknowledged my feelings for her, my relationship with my partner was over. Not simply because I anticipated being in a relationship with my friend, but because the introspection made me realize that I'd been slowly disengaging from my partner for a while. The spark just wasn't there. So I forced myself, finally, to be genuine and firm, and told my partner that I just knew that taking time to "work on things" would be fruitless. It was heartbreaking to admit that there was no hope, but I knew without a doubt that this was true. And so we began the tedious and agonizing process of disentangling our lives while keeping our kids' lives as stable as possible.

It didn't work out that way for her—she stayed in her relationship, and one of the conditions of mending her marriage was that she no longer have me in her life. I tried to put myself in her partner's shoes, but I was crushed. I both grieved the loss of my fourteen-year relationship that I'd thought would last forever, and mourned the loss of this dear friend, who had pushed me to ask myself so many hard questions that would change my life completely. It felt so unfair to have made this huge jump—based on the emotions, wants, and needs that she and I had talked about for hours and hours—and not to be able to tell her about it.

And still I skated. She left the league, the sport, the city, and I skated on—longer, harder, pushing myself. I needed this sport and these people more than I ever had before, and they did not let me down. When I had my kids with me (half-time), I kept it together, getting meals on the table and keeping daily routines intact. When I didn't, these women in my derby community kept me moving forward. They offered couches, food, drinks, coffee, kid care, and hours and hours of talking: dissecting everything that had happened and every possibility for the future. There was always another practice, another game, another meeting, and they made sure I was there: weak and wobbly for a while, and increasingly strong as I settled into my new normal.

About a year after my separation, I was playing an away game, with my mom and kids in the crowd, when I felt a sharp pain in my ankle. At half-time, I put some ice on it until it was time to hit the track again, and as we were driving home, I asked my mom to stop for some painkillers and more ice. By the time I unlaced my sneakers at home, my ankle was as wide as my calf and deep purple, green, and yellow. Sure it was just a funny twist, I opted not to take my kids to the emergency room with me and waited it out for the rest of the weekend until I dropped them at school Monday morning. Several hours and x-rays later, the slightly surprised doctor told me I had broken my fibula in the first five minutes of the game and would now be looking at life in a cast for six weeks or so. *Whatever,* I thought, *I'm incredibly self-sufficient, and I'm in really good shape—this'll be no sweat. Besides, I've always thought crutches were cool.*

I quickly learned that life with one leg is no small deal and leaned on my teammates once more: they drove me places, walked my kids to and from school, brought us meals, and dragged me along to watch practices to keep me motivated and my head in the game.

Kristi, a woman I knew peripherally in the league, was one of the first to offer to bring me a meal, and when she came by, I invited her in to join me while I ate. Being stranded at home (and completely alone when the kids were with their dad), I was anxious for company, and it seemed like a good opportunity to get to know her better. She'd always seemed funny, smart, and talented, but we'd never really talked much; our relationship was mostly confined to the derby venue. But that night, we really got to know each other, and after a lot of laughter, we made plans to get together again.

As time passed, I became comfortable with single parenthood and committed to the life I'd created for myself, postseparation. I loved being able to have my house set up exactly as I wanted it. I found that the time I spent with my kids was more meaningful.

And I continued to enjoy hours of derby. Dating didn't even cross my mind. My heart was still bruised after the year I'd just been through. So, while I was thrilled to have made a new friend, I certainly wasn't thinking that it would move toward romance. But after a few months of close friendship, carefully getting to know each other, I think we were both starting to feel a bit more sparkly about each other than we'd anticipated.

When she told me that she planned to go visit family for a couple of weeks, my heart leapt into my throat, feeling sick at the thought of being apart for that long.

But her time away brought things into focus. Over the course of countless texts and phone calls, she decided to come home a bit early. This would be the beginning of us.

We were both nervous about what it would be like to cross this line. But when she returned, we raced into each other's arms—and headed off to practice. Afterward, she came over, and we spent the night together.

I almost wept.

I had felt like I could have lived the rest of my life just not that interested in sex. I was sad that it had taken such a dramatic upheaval and such loss to get me to understand that I did, in fact, want and need a sexual relationship—it just needed to be different than the one I'd had. I wished I had been braver. I wished I had understood and had said earlier, "I want more, and it's not you, but this isn't right for me." But it didn't play out that way. While I was glad that I had gotten to this new place, my heart hurt when I thought of how I'd gotten there.

But we skated through this, too—through the turbulence and into the calm. We packed each other's bags, bandaged each other's wounds, pushed each other when we felt too tired to go on. We came home together—eyes bright, adrenaline pumping—and sat on the couch, devouring whatever food we could get our hands on, debriefing every drill, every move, every decision, until we couldn't possibly stay awake any longer. Then we would crawl into bed, wrap around each other and sleep.

While I still grieve the relationships lost, I rejoice in the love I found. And I thank my lucky stars for roller derby, too, in all of its imperfect glory. None of this would have happened without those skates, that concrete, and my league. When I had no idea where things were going, I knew exactly what would happen at practice: my teammates would clear a path for me, push me through, and protect me from anyone trying to stop me from getting where I wanted to be.

Unexpected Expedition

BY K. ASTRE

I THOUGHT I KNEW, BUT I WASN'T SURE, SO I WAITED. Almost like when you suspect something has gone bad in the fridge. You notice that the food has been in there a long time, but you put off dealing with it until a later time when you're less busy or less overwhelmed. You check the expiration date but doubt the accuracy of its timing. Then you sniff. Smells fine. You think. What does sour cream smell like, anyway? But then you taste it, and the bitterness has depth, like it's been incubating, germinating. Exactly how long has this been in here, you wonder, to achieve this level of rot, to reach this height of denial?

I may not have been able to solve the rudimentary riddle of rotting, but I learned that, like food, identities can also lose shape, quality, and flavor the longer they remain uninspected.

For many years I didn't know what else to call myself but bisexual. During and immediately following college, I dated women but it was casual, light-hearted, short term, and in between stints with semi-serious boyfriends. I had no plans of growing old with these girls. We had never exchanged declarations of forever. In fact, we didn't intend to introduce one another to our parents or families, ever. Although my experiences with men had never been entirely satisfying emotionally, I had every intention of marrying a man, having children, and living my life in the convenient, if not constraining, comforts of compulsory heterosexuality.

I learned about men the way children learn about most things—through observations at home, out in the world, and on screen. I tried to find another way to understand men outside of them being generally burdensome to the women around them. Women got the short end of the stick—they cooked, cleaned, reared children, and worked while begging their male counterparts for empathy, emotional support, and to take out trash or clean the toilet without being asked.

A lot of men seemed to get away with being innocently chauvinistic providers who acted as the head of household yet rarely contributed to the actual care of the home or family unit. I didn't want to believe in the narrative of the permanently adolescent man, but it seemed inescapable. Though I had every intention of getting married and having a traditional marriage, I fantasized that after my children had grown up and gone to college, I would find a nice woman to settle down with. Only after my politely homophobic parents died, of course.

I couldn't stand the idea of my parents disowning me or being disappointed by my decision to spend my life with a woman. During my elementary school obsession with the Spice Girls, I made it my mission to watch every performance I could catch. I sat eagerly in the living room, absorbing all the girl power, as my dad came in and out of the room. Often their background dancers were men, and my dad rarely missed an opportunity to make fun of them because he assumed they were gay. His comments, smirks, scoffs, and snickers told me that he would not approve of me unless I was straight.

I was already Black and fat—two items on the infinite list of attributes that make it difficult to feel celebrated in America—and as an adult, I didn't have the mental or emotional capacity to broadcast romantic love for another woman. It would make me even more of a target. Psychologically, I was just not prepared to weather the cultural consequences of exposing another layer of my identity. I grew up believing the world saw gay people as confused, traumatized, mentally ill, or evil. It wasn't just my dad. I wasn't just afraid of being ostracized by my religious family and embarrassing my god-fearing mother. I felt like the world at large would reject me.

I allowed myself to be led by societal expectations. This was easy; it didn't require any mental or emotional introspection, nor did it require any profound examination. I found a nice but deeply troubled young man who loved me as much as he needed me, and as we dated we made plans to do what people our age did: move in together, get engaged, stay happily married, raise a family. Though I often felt like something nameless was missing, I forged on. He was as sweet and as accommodating as I figured any man could be. I hadn't witnessed very much gentlemanly conduct growing up; my expectations for chivalry were admittedly low. He opened doors for me, carried my bags, loved my cooking, held my hand at every opportunity, and was proud to be with me. I didn't think there was much else to ask for out of a relationship because I didn't know what heights my senses could scale.

And then I met Theary, an openly gay woman, at a meditation retreat. There was an electricity between us that I had never felt before. Not because it was new and exciting, but because it was authentic. Theary exhilarated me. Her beautiful deep-brown skin, low-cut fade, and soft, full body moved me.

Our friendship continued after the retreat, but I was desperate for more. She made regular cameos in my dreams, sometimes walking through them like an omen. My need to belong to her took over. It was the sweetest possession I had ever known. I was attracted to her boldness, her confidence, and her insistence that the world accept her as she is. We sent each other poems and journal entries. I was blindsided by the intensity of my desire. While my anxieties remained, I couldn't control my emotions, couldn't find an internal compartment vast enough to stuff the sensations back into, even if I wanted to. That's when I knew I had to break up with *him* and tell *her* exactly how I was feeling.

Theary and I spent a lot of time together following my confession. One day after coffee, her car suddenly stopped working. We called roadside assistance and talked in the car while we waited. Hours passed, and I could feel something changing. A sweetness settled in between us. I was struck by the depth of our connection, the richness of our conversations, the density of our desire. Our world together was kaleidoscopic. That evening, after she dropped me off at home, she texted me something that changed everything: "I fell in love with you today."

I had already fallen in love with her, but her admission inspired me to unfold and investigate myself in a way I had never allowed. I discovered, to my delight, a woman within myself who had the courage to live authentically and honestly, and who would give herself permission to love another woman. Though I had found a place of acceptance within myself, I still had no idea what was to come. I realized I had no compass, no map, and no directions for how to move forward.

I came out in tender, timid layers. First, to my family. The day I decided to come out to my mother, I was ready to shed my fear. I called her in the afternoon while she was at work and abruptly told her that I had a girlfriend. She was quiet for a while. She sighed. I paced around my living room, waiting for her to say something. Finally, she calmly started asking me questions. I was so relieved by her tone. She was curious and confused, but not angry or upset. She wanted to know some basics, like when I became interested in women, but most importantly, why I had never told her. She blamed herself, worried that my lifestyle was a result of not having many positive male role models in my youth. As a child, I was surrounded by women. Intelligent, beautiful, innovative, resilient, strong-willed, trailblazing women who served as an example of the type of supportive, loyal, responsible, and emotionally present partner that anyone—man or woman—would want to be with. But that was not the reason.

"I've found someone that I want to spend the rest of my life with," I said.

Next, I came out to my friends and colleagues. I felt liberated, lost, relieved, petrified, enlivened.

My relationship with Theary evolved quickly. We moved in together. The intimacy of sharing space made us grow closer than ever. Everything was magical—from eating dinner to running errands—just because we were together. On one trip to the store, we were having a conversation about how delighted we were to have found each other. We were so immersed in our talk that we parked and stayed in the car for almost an hour. Then one of us (in such a blur of emotion, I can't remember which) blurted out, "Let's just get married right now!"

The tone of the conversation changed from whimsical to serious. This was something we both wanted, although we soon realized we had definitely gotten carried away. We made a pact with each other that if we still wanted to get married by the next Valentine's Day, we would.

And we did. Our ceremony took place in our backyard in front of some of our family and closest friends. Committing to a lifelong partnership with my wife was an act of both rising in truth and plunging deeper into the folds of my true self. My mother and father sat in the front row on our special day, smiling and being as supportive as they could.

Haitian Kompa and R&B songs played in the background as laughs and happy voices filled the air after the ceremony. Throughout the evening, I caught my mom smiling at me and watching with so much love in her eyes. When I had a moment to myself, she pulled me aside.

"I am so proud of you, dear," she said.

"Oh, Mom . . . "

"No, I really am. All I want is for you to be happy, even if that means your father and I have to be a little uncomfortable. We will deal with our own feelings, but what's most important is that you live your life. That's all we care about."

"Thank you, Mom. I'm very happy," I assured her.

"I can tell."

Sometimes I felt like I had tainted the relationship I had with my parents by not being honest with them earlier, but Mom's blessing showed there was room for growth in our relationship because of her unconditional love. Tears welled up in her eyes as she hugged me for a long time. My dad spotted us embracing and came over, smiling.

"Hey, I want a hug, too," he teased.

We laughed as we opened our arms to him. I was glad I hadn't waited until my parents were gone to live my fantasy life. My truthfulness had transformed us all—individually and collectively.

When Did You Know?

BY TRISH BENDIX

WHEN DID YOU KNOW YOU WERE STRAIGHT?

Was it in preschool? When playtime meant the girls baked in the pretend kitchenettes and the boys were given rubber balls and you made believe you were your mother, making dinner for your dad because that's just what you do? Or was it in kindergarten when you watched Disney movies where the happy ending came in the form of a long-awaited kiss from a charming prince? Was it when the neighborhood boys told you to meet them behind the garage and dared you to show them your privates before they'd show you theirs?

Maybe it was in first grade when recess was dedicated to chasing boys with your friends. Or every Ken doll purchased for Barbie or Skipper and her friends, so they had someone to impress.

It could have been the New Kids on the Block—having to pick one of the boy-band members to be the focus of your adoration. Then you'd kiss his face on your pillow and your wall before you went to sleep and dream of the day you could finally meet and maybe even hold hands. He'd sing you a love song with his impressive falsetto, and you'd feel like you were the most special girl in all of the world because he chose *you*.

Perhaps it was in middle school, when real boyfriends replaced girls' celebrity fantasies. Your friends were suddenly so grown up, with bras and periods and parties where their parents weren't home. Expectations became different. Songs were more sensual. You went to the mall with your friend and she changed in the bathroom—she brought a shirt that shows off her stomach, and her underwear was strategically poking out of the top of her low-rise jeans. You'd walk around in loops looking for boys that went to different schools—maybe even high schools.

Was it at the teen dance club where you could be thirteen or fourteen and tell anyone who asked that you were seventeen? When you felt lucky that an older guy wanted to dance with you and then secretly scared when he danced too close and invited you to a party at his friend's house afterward, or embarrassed when you had to tell him no because your mom was picking you up, or mortified when he said, "Excuse me, I have to use the bathroom," and you saw him a few minutes later dancing with another girl?

Confirmation could have come when everyone coupled up for homecomings and proms and you wanted to be asked because it meant something if you weren't. You said yes to someone you barely knew and felt uncomfortable when he decided you'd drive separately from the rest of your friends. He dropped you off early so he could go out and party and you felt like you must be some buzzkill.

But then you finally had a boyfriend—someone who was into the same kinds of things as you: music, theater, family, friends. And yet the only thing you shared was interests. It wasn't anything like the movies had promised—sparks, fireworks, butterflies. You tried to make things happen so you wouldn't have empty answers for your inquiring friends, but it never felt good, and once while you were kissing, he stopped, telling you he was bored. You were devastated, but only because you felt inadequate, like you were doing something wrong. It all felt wrong.

You moved away to the big city to go to college, where you knew you were destined to meet the kind of guy you'd connect with: the Prince Charming, Jordan Knight, Ken doll you'd been promised since you were old enough to know what your future looked like. And you kept trying. You went to classes and parties and met all kinds of new and different people—and there was that one girl who, for some reason, you saw and thought *I want to know her.* She just walked right into the auditorium and found a seat that wasn't next to yours, but you could still watch her from where you sat, elevated, and wondered about her—her crooked nose, her effortless cool, her pierced lip, her loose curls dyed a shade of sun-tinged pink, like the color of a tongue after licking a dreamsicle.

It took a while, but eventually your paths crossed and you became friends, and you never thought you'd have so much fun with someone. Together you'd write silly songs—she was a real musician—and try to find albums that matched perfectly with movies on mute. When the lyrics and the moment synced like a surprise soundtrack, it gave you both so much satisfaction—although maybe it was the weed.

Not yet old enough to drink, twenty-four-hour diners and coffee shops were worth the walk, even in the cruelest of Chicago winters, and you found yourself jealous when she gave the tattooed server a mix tape, but you didn't understand why.

You'd play Tegan and Sara albums and Never Have I Ever and Truth or Dare, and when you were dared to kiss her, you liked it so much, you wanted to play all the time. You wanted to play alone, and you didn't want her to invite guys over like she sometimes did. And then she turned twenty-one, and things changed. She got a new roommate, started going out more, leaving you young and confused about why you felt so hurt and abandoned.

It wasn't long after that that you met another girl who put you under a similar spell. You realized you weren't who you'd assumed yourself to be, and things started to make a new kind of sense. You were less lonely. You understood why, for twenty years, you felt out of touch with the world and what it was supposed to be for you, and what you were supposed to be in it. Love seemed possible, like something you could finally give and receive in a way you'd longed to, though you'd never quite known how.

Other moments presented themselves in retrospect, clues that you'd somehow missed—like your fascination with your unmarried English teacher who came to school some days crying about the terrible fights she'd had with her "roommate." Or how you skipped your senior prom to go see your favorite singer play her band's last gig—oh, how you loved watching her on stage. You even interviewed her for the school paper and inquired if she had a boyfriend. It was so disappointing that the answer was yes.

You fit into some stereotypes, playing soccer and softball and basketball and having intense, close friendships with other girls on the team. One, in particular. You were each other's dates to most dances and traveled together for spring break, spending a week together, sleeping in the same bed—until a huge blow-up fight that left you both heartbroken, walking solemnly side by side at graduation and not talking for years.

But even before that, you would read your grandma's *True Story* magazines and pore over the advertisements for women's bathing suits. The busty models posed in bikinis and high-cut one-pieces in monochrome colors, stirring something in you that you didn't want to consider.

Later, you somehow stumbled upon some erotica about lesbian cheerleaders, thanks to the Internet. Still, you didn't question what it meant that it turned you on. It was sex—it was sexy. That was enough. That's all it was. Sexuality is a spectrum, after all, you convinced yourself.

Benign things, though, that weren't about sex, but instead about rightness—those were things you knew you supported. In speech class, you gave a passionate talk about support for gay people, but didn't consider yourself one. You debated on behalf of a group you didn't think you belonged to, yet it was something you felt so strongly about that it emanated from your core, and anyone who dared question the truth of what was right was wrong for attempting the challenge. That's how you saw it. That's what you believed.

There was that movie, though: *But I'm a Cheerleader.* Something about that girl in the black button-down shirt. She summoned something that made you nervous to be watching her, like someone could walk in any second and accusingly ask what you were watching and why, even if it was just a still frame of her face. This was the first movie you'd ever seen with someone like her as the object of affection, of wanting. You'd seen covers for things like *Bound* at the local Blockbuster, but you'd been too young, too nervous to ever try and rent them. Still, curiosity was there, and you'd stumbled upon Clea DuVall on a premium cable network and she was saying she liked girls and then she was dancing with a girl, kissing a girl, having what could only be assumed was sex with a girl—damn those censors and the need to keep things so ambiguous and darkly lit, flashes of sapphism and orgasm and hands and mouths and caresses of the abdomen.

All of these things—signs, symbols, clues—were still so easy to ignore because an option to be something other than a girl looking for her boy did not exist. Gay was something only boys could be; gay was something you knew from the day you were born. Gay was an identity you were certain of, a statement, not a question. Right? *Right?* Right?

But then you asked yourself, and it was the first time anyone had ever posed the question—might as well be you. *Am I straight?*

The question is scary; the answer scarier. The alternative is hiding, lying, denying, something you're just not able to. Because now you're really sitting with yourself, knowing yourself, and finding that the answer is *no*.

You are not the thing you thought you were, that everyone else wants you to be. And they can't help it, because that's what was wanted for them, predestined without much thought, really. It's just The Way Things Are.

Not for you, though. You are faced with something different, something no one else in your family seems to have ever had to wonder about themselves, because they have always been able to answer "when did you know you were straight?" with every feeling they've ever had, every minute that's passed, every experience they've lived. And you have questions, questions that seemed to have no logical answers until now, because you are actually asking yourself the right one: *Am I gay?*

It's instantly inescapable. You know it as soon as you ask; there's no need to try harder with men—you're not "selling yourself short" as your mom will offer. "Gay" isn't a consolation prize you've given yourself because you haven't found "the right guy."

Who are you? you ask. And you're young, but what you do know now, for sure—because nothing has ever felt more like a predetermined, clear, and exciting discovery for you—is that you are gay. You are a lesbian. You deserve love just the same as you always have. And now that you know this and love this about yourself, the world will know this and love this, too.

You realize it might take time. Maybe it will take twenty more years. But things will reinforce this answer, this truth, for you; things will assure you and guide you throughout your life. Some people's answers may shift or flow or change, but all you needed was that question.

When did you know you were straight?
The answer is never.

Here's to Me

BY JEANNOT JONTE BOUCHER

GRAND PRAIRIE, TEXAS, IS HOME. IT'S A LIVED-IN WORKING-class suburb of Dallas where Spanish is heard more often in the grocery store than English. Grand Prairie's Immaculate Conception Catholic Church had a glass room at the back for mothers to sit with crying children, the Cry Box. This way, the children wouldn't disturb other parishioners during mass.

Nearly ten years ago, I felt fortunate to have a way to participate in my faith in this tangle of babies and toddlers who nursed and pinched us, dug in our purses, and played with our keys. I loved to have a place to sing the hymns, which made me feel connected to something bigger than myself; to sing an old song in harmony feels like community to me. On the other side of the glass, in the back row, sat nuns in traditional black habits. I watched them kneel. I didn't attempt it, seven months pregnant. I was twenty, almost twenty-one. As I held my toddler's hand and tried to keep her from running laps around the Cry Box, the crying around us drowned out the singing of the Pater Noster, *Our Father, who art in heaven, hallowed be thy name.*

My husband, James, sat next to me. There were no other fathers. He looked tired.

I was at times aware of my unhappiness, and other times I felt the weight of suffering that comes with being a woman, but I heard the priest's homily over the Cry Box speaker: "Wasn't it suffering that redeemed our souls?" Couldn't I offer this small suffering in prayer? I begged my soul for patience, impatient with my own unease with the woman's role. The homily continued, but my attention wandered. Why was I here, living like this? It was a discontent sometimes as small and persistent as the itching of a sweater, other times so vast and profound that I felt incapacitated. After mass, I stood in front of the statue of Our Lady of Guadalupe, looking at her starry blue and gold mantle and her lowered eyes. If you had asked me what was wrong at that moment, I could have told you that everything was wrong—or, if I lied, that nothing was wrong. In the car, I confessed to my husband I'd rather stay home the next Sunday.

When I was a teenager, I had loved the Roman Catholic faith for giving me answers about the world. The complex philosophical systems gave me a framework in which to begin young adulthood. I had answers that the Church Fathers had written about in extreme detail. It seemed unchanging through the ages, like a rock, an anchor. When peers wrestled with questions of sexuality, abortion, marriage, family, the Consecrated Sisters taught me that humility and obedience were good for a woman's soul. Part of me was at least initially relieved not to worry about so many difficult questions. But that relief was slowly displaced by a quiet pain, a loud warning—a sign that something was very wrong.

In my early twenties, with two babies, I was alone so often: while I nursed them or put them down for naps or prayed and rocked them while they cried. "Nearer my God, to thee, nearer to thee," I sang, listening to Christian radio to hear another voice in my home while my husband worked early and then late shifts. Every morning I made sure to tune in to Ave Maria radio, to listen to husband-and-wife relationship coaches giving faith-based counsel. With my hands busy in the warm water as I washed dishes, I became fixated: a young man had called in to ask the couple holiday advice regarding a homosexual relative. The wife advised, "Oh no, you can't send that message that their sin is acceptable in the eyes of the Lord by letting him in your home during the holiday. Send a firm message that you cannot condone the sin of homosexuality in your home. Not until he is willing to disavow his lifestyle." I dropped my favorite holiday dish, a yellow-edged one with blueberries. My throat felt tight; I could hear my pulse and feel my face getting hot. If I could close my eyes tightly enough, I wouldn't be able to cry, I thought. My mother told me if you touch your tongue to the roof of your mouth, no tears will come out. The clatter of the falling dish woke my younger baby after a hard-won nap.

Staying home with a newborn and a toddler, I counted the minutes until my husband would be home from work. The whole day of chores stretched backwards. I read magazines for mothers and books about babies, and after one of them ran a blurb about lesbian mothers and children's well-being, I got the wildest hair to go to the library's LGBT resource center and learn more about the perspectives of those outside my faith and what their lives might be like. The relationship coach's advice about homosexuals and the holiday was in my heart. I could say the interest sprung from nowhere, but I was the kind of teen who fell in love with best friends, who were sometimes girls. I took it as the gift of holy grace that I had been able to follow the Church's doctrine on sexuality and marry according to teaching. But, still, there was some nagging question in me. I knew what St. Thomas Aquinas wrote about morbid curiosity, that it was a sin. Regardless, I packed the diaper bag and drove off on an adventure. Plus, there would be people at the library, and for a stay-at-home mom, that was as big a draw as any.

I brought the babies in with me, one in a tummy pack strapped above my long skirt and sleeves, and introduced myself to a librarian. I asked if they could help me get a book I had read about in a magazine. "What book might that be?" she asked. I glanced around the room to see who was looking, then pronounced the title: *Dear John, I Love Jane: Women Write about Leaving Men for Women.*

"Of course, I love my husband," I explained, "and have no intention of leaving him, but I just, well, I would like to know about those stories."

When it came in, I devoured the stories while I breastfed and stew simmered in the crock pot—the routine in those days. The women in the book had been sad, and they hadn't known why. Like . . . me?

When James came home, I invited him to sit with me on the couch to talk. He cocked his head at the unusually formal invitation. In little more than a whisper, I explained that I didn't want to go back to Immaculate Conception another Sunday—or ever. I felt emboldened after saying something so impossible. His eyebrows raised with curiosity, waiting for an explanation.

"I would like an open relationship," I said, "to be able to see a woman." He sighed and left the room. He had never been the kind of man whose emotions were easy to read, but this time I heard exasperation and avoidance in his sigh. I couldn't be dismissed. Not this time.

I followed him and told him breathlessly about the stories I had read, women who found happiness going on a few dates, and how "we could still be a happy family." He looked at his computer screen while I spoke, as I tried to get his attention back. "It would be nice to know someone like me who—" and then a baby woke up, and the toddler poured a big bucket of dog food all over the floor.

I waited for him to be ready. Without pestering, every few weeks, I asked if I might be able to make a dating profile online and just go for coffee with a girl. The librarian at the LGBT center made me fascinating stacks of books, like *The Paradox of Natural Mothering,* where I learned about women who gave and gave to their families but left nothing for themselves. She gave me *The Second Sex* by Simone de Beauvoir, and while I fed and dandled the children on my knee, between planting roses and herbs in the garden, I pondered how I was this *other* kind of being, and man came first. One thing led to another in these books, and I started exploring the LGBT library on my own. I found a cracked paperback, *Androgyne,* 1976, and I read a description of this androgyne, a soul of worlds within worlds. I copied down the words of this book, handwritten, because they sounded like me. At lightning speed, and all alone except for the babies, I tore through countless pages, seeking something. Longing.

Eventually my husband gave me permission to see women—after I stormed into his office and demanded it. If I couldn't be free to determine who I could love or touch, I had no business in this marriage. He didn't say much, but he suggested I was eaten up with postpartum depression, and I had been reading too many feminist books. I told him I meant it, that I needed this. I wanted to be fierce and smash everything that held me back, but instead, my eyes implored him. "Please, James," I finally begged, "I need this—or I have to go." Whether it was the pestering or the ultimatum neither of us wanted, he finally agreed.

There was a date or two for coffee or to the city gardens during the day, but with the small children coming along with me, I felt too burdened to enjoy myself. I had work to do in the evenings after all, cooking and serving and getting clothes ironed for the next day. The best I could hope for was to spend the day with another mother friend with babies and cook and clean together, even though we were sweet on each other. When this mother friend and I developed an affection, our husbands found it a little charming, and they remarked over a communal dinner that we girls seemed entertained. I remember one evening, after we had made our husbands a sumptuous tortilla soup, we carried the babies to a bedroom together to nurse them to sleep. In the dark, we held hands. I caressed her face, and her smooth chin was like silk. Did the touch fill her soul with light and warmth the way it did mine? Was this soul like mine? Moments like this, my soul magnified. I could close my eyes and savor, until the babies were asleep, and we could try to slip away from their dimpled arms, which would grasp for us again if we got up too quickly. Between visits with the other wife, I read Anaïs Nin's novel, *Ladders to Fire*, and I watched queer period drama, like the WWII love story between the wife of a German officer and a Jewish lesbian, *Aimée and Jaguar*.

One night I was scrolling through social media when I saw an advertisement for a queerlesque variety show at the local lesbian bar. My god, what could that even be? I asked my friend if I could borrow ten dollars from her to go to the show. (My thirty-five-dollars-a-month personal allowance was long gone through due to my gardening hobby.) My husband gave me permission to go. When I put the children to bed, I changed into a short, sequined dress and heels, something I had almost no occasion to do. It was so strange to be alone in the car at night! But I was a feminist now, and I should be. I turned the music up loud.

There was an upstairs theater with heavy red-velvet curtains. The room was completely packed. Many of the women were dressed up like pinup models and covered in vintage flash tattoos of birds and nude women. These pompadoured and pin-curled and victory-rolled femmes linked their arms with androgynous . . .

boyfriends? Butches? I wasn't sure. I'd learned the word gender-queer before that night; I'd seen photos of androgynous folks who played with fluid gender expression; I knew some were trans, and some weren't. And they inspired my imagination. I felt a spark. I even told my husband over dinner, "I must be genderqueer, too," to which he had nodded and changed the subject.

At that moment in the theater, I found a stool at the back, by myself, and felt cast into another world—like I had walked through a portal. Beautiful drag queens read their original poetry. Voluptuous women sang torch songs. A red-haired emcee lit candles for someone in the community who had been lost. *The community*, she pronounced in her speech. The words echoed in me as someone passed me a candle to light.

And then she walked on stage. The colored lights above her shone through a gauzy-blue antique nightgown with lace around the neck. I had never seen anyone so visually striking. Through the veil of the cloth, I could see outlines of her skin beneath, which looked tender and femininely soft but strong, even from the distance. Her dark hair in finger waves reminded me of Jaguar, from the movie. It was like stepping into the films I had only watched alone. She was tall, close to seven feet in her towering heels, with huge green eyes and full lips. Everything about her was on a grand scale—yet she appeared, to me, so vulnerable.

The piano stage left was hers. She sat down on the lone stool and told us she would sing a song she had just written, "Here's to Me." It was melancholy and touching, catchy and funny. She sang about being a transgender woman and feeling so alone:

> *Here's to sitting and crying alone in the hall over not*
> *   really filling that dress out at all*
> *Here's to raising my wrist, having never been kissed.*
> *Here's to being eleven feet tall.*
> *Here's to kneeling and praying along without saying a*

word about what I believed
Here's to answering questions with constant denial
Here's to wearing my heart on my sleeve—

The crowd cheered and whooped, even more when she came out again in a corset to play the accordion, then the upright bass, stepping her foot on the pedal of the hi-hat cymbal like a one-person theater of music.

I told my husband every detail about the night, especially about Ashley, the performer, until he said, "Stop talking." It was too late for the religious teachings to control me. I held onto the vision from the night before. *Whatever God there could be loves this woman,* I thought, *and anyone who could say that's wrong doesn't know anything about the universe. There is something more, something beautiful, and I've seen it. I've been there.*

I yielded to the obsession of thinking about her and disregarded any distant worries about salvation, temptation, Satan. *If I could just see her again,* I thought. I found her profile online and discovered more shows coming up. I splurged without permission: twenty dollars to see her perform in a Cirque du Burlesque at a historic theater. There would be acrobats on aerial silks and burlesque stars. I found a photo of her singing in the theater posted by a local photographer, and I asked if I could buy a poster. *My favorite local singer,* I told myself. But I was already in love with her.

I had responsibilities—a husband to keep happy for my own preservation, children to care for, a home to maintain. I had only just started working outside the home as a first grade teacher. Over a dinner of pot pies, James got quieter, then asked me to bring him a tray in his office alone. *James,* I reasoned, *I am not going to run off into the sunset with anyone.*

After that, he started taking more meals alone in his office.

As the children rolled and tickled around the bed past their sleep time, I wrote to her. "I do not know if you date women, or if you date married women, but I would like to date you. Would you like to go out?" And within minutes, to my astonishment, there was a reply. She said at first no, she didn't date anyone and hadn't for eleven years—not since high school. And she was transgender, she wrote, expecting that I would be concerned with that.

As soon as I got those babies to bed—and bedtime could not come fast enough—I wrote to her again, offering friendship, telling her that wherever she was—I was feeling grandiose—I would like to be, in whatever capacity she could share. And I told her that I was genderqueer, a kind of transgender, so maybe we had something in common? She wrote to me that she didn't know a lot of people and had been something of a shut-in for many years until so recently, and she would love to go out. What was there to lose, anyway? We decided on a walk through the city gardens. My husband was irritated about having to take care of the children in the middle of a Sunday morning, but I rushed out the door.

Following that morning, Ashley and I were nearly inseparable. For all the queer love stories I had watched and read about, that first date was more. On an iron bench in the gardens, we shared stories about our lives. I tried not to talk too much so that I would have more time to learn about her. But still, the chemistry was palpable. I tried to imagine what it would be like not to have shame about liking women. We were each so curious about the other. When she spoke to me, her hand would so casually touch me, as if it were nothing. To me, she was skipping rocks over a still pond, and the waves shook rings over me. When we left, I thanked her for being generous with her time, and if this would be our only meeting, I was so grateful for it. I smiled, closed lipped, and she looked horrified. "Oh no," she laughed, "Let's see each other many times." She then invited me to live readings by queer people in the community the next day.

She introduced me to what felt like a hundred fascinating artists, writers, musicians, and dancers. Before long, Ashley was having dinner with us four or five nights a week. She woke up in the guest bedroom with a four-year-old finger painting her leg. A two-year-old dropped a coconut macaroon on her pillow and dashed out of the room.

Over time, my husband and I each built, or rebuilt, notions of private faith apart from the Church. On our own, we explored personal visions of a faith with room to find more of our own answers. Certainly, when James became interested in dating, I supported him and encouraged him to explore. Unlike me, however, he didn't burn with eagerness to tell stories about who he saw. Being naturally more private, much remained and still remains a mystery to me. He never had much to say about me being genderqueer or wanting to pursue gender transition visibly. He would sigh and change the subject.

One day, my husband put his foot down. "This is too much," he said. "Which day of the week will you see Ashley?" At that moment, she knocked on the door. So, I *had* invited her to drop by again for a cup of tea on her way into the city, or perhaps coming here was out of the way, but was it really so bad if she was stopping by just so briefly? And she did need to drop off this small item she had borrowed? I smiled weakly at him and invited her in. Oh, that face. When we were together, I felt like I could touch a soul like mine. "No, come on," my husband reminded me in front of her, "say good-bye and doll up, because we have our own date tonight." It was a tense moment. I nodded dutifully and went to the bedroom to begin browsing clothing for a Mexican food dinner date without the children. During our prior date, we had strained conversation and commented too much on the enchiladas.

"Doll up," I whispered to myself, as tears welled in my eyes. The edges of my dresses seemed like sandpaper and fiberglass on my fingertips. I caught a glimpse of Ashley staring at me from just past the doorway.

She was studying me and put together all the pieces, faster than I did. I dolled up for him, for the church, for our parents. Sometimes, I did it for me, but mostly, I did it for approval. But in her gaze, I knew she saw something; we shared something about gender and who we were.

"Why do you love me?" she asked, feeling the mounting tension in our lives.

I paused.

"I found a novel at a sale once. I haven't even read it. But the title, the title is you, to me."

"What was the book called?"

"*At the Root of This Longing.*"

Tears began to blur her eyeliner. She held me in the bedroom before I got dressed for the date—with my husband. As I looked up at her before exiting my room, tears rolled down her blushed cheeks and into my eyes, like something out of a dark fairy tale. I wound her dark curls around my hands. We kissed, lingering, slow, like there would never be enough time in all creation.

I loved my husband, too. Looking back, the love I had with him had been so stilted by the roles taught to us in the church, and we were so burdened by parenting young that our youthful love was fraught with responsibilities and stress. What we could have been to each other never developed. What if we had not set out in marriage thinking I had to submit to his authority—and what if he hadn't believed it was his responsibility? The allowances, permissions, visions of the father as head of the household crumbled away without sermons about the necessity of that dynamic. Over time, most of the power dynamic did shift, but not quickly enough. Every now and then, something would pass that Ashley would notice. Every time James and I fell into old habits, like me serving and clearing his plate at dinner, or depositing my paycheck right into his account, it stood out as bizarre. No, even without the Catholic faith, tradition intruded. Love for Ashley wasn't enough to undo all of the ingrained patterns with my husband.

One night, James walked into the living room when Ashley and I were up late laughing on the couch together, when—we thought—everyone in the family was asleep. We kissed and touched, pausing to smile and talk.

"Where do you want to be buried one day?" I asked her conversationally, curled into the spoon of her body.

"Bury me in you," she replied.

Yet, there was James, a few feet away, in the shadows. How long had he been watching? His slumped shoulders of disappointment erased my smile, and my throat tightened. I felt a prickly heat of shame to see realization pass over his face. Part of me was ashamed I had made my husband unhappy.

"You are not this happy with me," he said the following day. "It's time for me to go."

I begged him to stay. I wasn't ready. I clung to some dream of happiness we had shared years ago, as teenagers wanting a family. Things had changed. I wanted, against reality, for us to all be able to live together as a family. Maybe I could have him and Ashley in a family, and I wouldn't have to give anyone up? In *Dear John, I Love Jane,* one of the writers had a husband who stayed close to them and moved only a block away! In such denial, I toured a rental house a block away, sure he must still love me— and a separation isn't a divorce, right? But, to marry Ashley was such a thing beyond dreaming—I indulged the daydream even if I thought I might not ever get to have such a wish come true.

These days, I looked so different from the year I first met her. My hair was all cut off, and a child in passing remarked to me that I used to look so much like a princess and now so much like a cowboy. When I started insisting that my husband call me *Johnny* like my new friends did in the queer community, he finally said, "It's all too much," and with bitterness, "After all these changes, what's next?"

On Mother's Day, he left permanently.

On Mother's Day, Ashley and I searched our souls for why we needed each other more than anything in the world—for our very survival. Ashley planted a blossoming redbud tree with me in our backyard, to represent her promise to mother the children with me. I searched for the meaning of Mother's Day, when I'd started cringing at being called a mother and knew viscerally that female pronouns and names were not right for me. Ashley understood my gender evolution almost without words. I wish this could have been a time to celebrate a new beginning together, but I was inconsolable. I was resentful of the glares we got in town when we were dropping the kids off, and crestfallen about slurs, and my parents' refusal to answer the phone when I called.

When we discovered my divorce was more than we could afford, that James had filed a suit for sole custody of our children, and that the court and CPS had questions about "a man dressed as a woman in the house with the children," we felt near completely crushed. But one of the few things that kept us going were songs. Ashley knew many of the old hymns from being the daughter of a church organist, and we sang together in harmony. Any old songs, really. The music healed me, as much as her presence. Genderqueer—and then I started using the word transgender more often for myself, too. As my voice changed, we kept singing.

We made a little name for ourselves singing duets and harmonies in queer bars and shows. We became a big part of the community, which had once been only a dream to me. We met hundreds, even thousands, of the queer people in the city, all stretched so thin, but coming out to support each other and cheer and throw a few dollars. Community and music nourished us, and as we gained strength, we gave back all we could to begin speaking and writing, to help others.

I don't look much like a woman at all, anymore. I'm ready to share the sides of myself no one else could see—except for Ashley that day in my bedroom when it hurt so much to put on makeup for a date—when she saw those worlds within worlds. The children call us both by our first names now at home—Johnny and Ashley. They hear us talk about gender often enough that they understand and follow our lead: You have to listen to what your soul needs, children. It's sometimes a small voice, but it's there.

We don't use the word lesbian, although some people used it to describe us when we got married. News crews arrived, alleging ours was a loophole lesbian marriage before same-sex marriage was legal in Texas. These days, words like gay and lesbian don't seem enough for us. On the street, some people call us a slur for men, others a slur for women. But in the queer community, we are loved.

It feels like a dare to have a teaching career now in Texas, fully in the public eye as a queer transgender family. I tried at first to keep it under wraps, but I couldn't stop going out with Ashley to speak at meetings, conferences, and do the work to help more people in the community. Eventually, my face was on the front of the newspaper, along with the huge words *Transgender Battle*. If anyone hadn't known, they did after that. I used to think that being myself would mean I could never be a teacher, but I think it makes me a better teacher. I know what it means to overcome expectations, to be told who and what you can be in this world, to find the courage to resist and keep asking for what you need.

Ashley and I remember the pain of feeling isolated and alone, and we want to make our home and our work a space for people to find each other. With the change in political climate coming, we are adjusting our sails to help the community stay close and in mutual support.

When we touch, the story of men and women in discrete categories sounds like a game someone else is playing—a game we both had to play for our survival, long ago. But when we are alone, I know I am with a soul like mine. I may call her *she,* and she may call me *he,* but *we* are safe. We are the same kind. One of our friends laughed that we like to sit on the fence of gender together, with our legs hanging off opposite sides. But we look at each other.

Four years together now, she pours me a little glass of wine after we make our way through bus pickups and homework and tuck our kids into bed. She's the one special soul who sang *Here's to Me* in that blue gown and caught what some ineffable part of me needed to grow.

"Why do you love me?" she asks, "after all you've given away and changed?"

"You're still at the root of all this longing," I toast her. "Here's to us."

Spring Weddings, Australian Style

BY RUTH DAVIES

IN THE AUSTRALIAN SPRING OF 2016, WHEN I HAD PLANTED sunflowers for the first time and was delighting in the blooms opening, Elizabeth Gilbert announced that the end of her marriage to a man was due to her realization that she was in love with her—female—best friend of fifteen years, Rayya Elias. Elias has pancreatic cancer, and that diagnosis made Gilbert face the difference between loving someone and being in love with them. Her announcement was long and apologetic, using phrases such as "something which I hope and trust you will receive with grace" and "please understand . . . . I trust you are all sensitive enough to understand how difficult this has been." She explained that because she lives in the public eye, she has to tell the truth publicly.

I felt elation, at first, for the brief glimpse into new love and, selfishly, for the value that such a high-profile relationship can lend to the acceptance of my own. Then I was sad about the tragedy of it. Then I was annoyed at how deferential she seemed to feel she needed to be, in the face of everything else going on for her and Elias and for their families. If she had left her husband for another man, there would be less of a need for the summer of silence while they all came to terms with presenting this new status to a judgmental public.

Just a week before Gilbert's anouncement, my partner of more than ten years and I had attended the wedding of close friends of ours. My partner had been working overseas for the previous few months and it was going to be wonderful to have her home for a few days. Guests gathered in a small park overlooking Brisbane's Story Bridge on a perfect spring day, and we took the opportunity to catch up with other friends of the couple whom we hadn't seen for a while and to meet people we had been hearing about, or who had been hearing about us, for years but somehow hadn't met. People mingled, laughed, admired the banksias blooming and talked about the jacarandas that would soon provide a canopy of purple flowers over the park. Then the celebrant called for us to come together, and we watched while the bride and groom walked down the footpath towards us, hand in hand, smiling at each other, at us, at the day. At love. We listened while the celebrant welcomed all of us, no matter our beliefs. Then we listened to him marry them, with the words legally required in Australia that state marriage is the union of a man and a woman, to the exclusion of all others.

The original *Marriage Act 1961* had a stance against exclusionary definitions, but in 2004, conservative Prime Minister John Howard rushed through an amendment to the Act, specifically to protect Australia from the rising tide of marriage equality that had begun in other countries: the Netherlands in 2001, Belgium in 2003 and in various U.S. states. The government wanted to lock down the definition of marriage not only within Australia, but to ensure that same-sex marriages in other countries could not be recognized as legal here.

Since 2004, things have improved. In 2008 and 2009, Prime Minister Kevin Rudd introduced reforms that gave equal entitlements and responsibilities to same-sex couples that de facto and married couples already had in areas of federal jurisdiction, such as social security, citizenship, taxation, and superannuation. In some ways, these changes have made me complacent about same-sex marriage, as it seems that in my relationship, we already have the legal recognition we need. However, some state laws also govern aspects of relationships, and these laws don't all provide full equality. In most states, gay and lesbian relationships are recognized through civil partnerships or by granting most of the same rights as de facto relationships have. But in a case in South Australia, a British couple—two men—were honeymooning in Adelaide, when one of them died. Their marriage was not recognized in the state, and the surviving partner had to hand over all decisions about the funeral and other matters to his father-in-law. This reminded me that the only way to guarantee full equality is to provide same-sex couples with the option of marriage. Marriage is a federal law in Australia—so that is where the battle for marriage equality must be fought.

Across the same years that support for marriage equality has continued to grow, federal politics in Australia have had a period of unprecedented instability, where social issues—not least, the issue of marriage equality—have been used as bargaining chips in party-room politics. The most recent of these was in 2015, when yet another leadership spill delivered Malcolm Turnbull, our fifth Prime Minister in six years. I roared with laughter when it happened, being particularly affronted by the outgoing PM, but I hadn't realized the cost: a previous election promise had to be kept of having a plebiscite on same-sex marriage. A plebiscite is an expensive way of being seen to consult the whole electorate, without having to enact the voters' decision. And it provides a platform for bigotry that will be damaging to people who are already vulnerable, particularly LGBTQ youth. Suicide rates among gay youth are up to six times higher than among their heterosexual peers. My children are now in their early twenties; I look at them and wonder how they feel about this. What is going on inside, under the discussions that we have about it? Hannah Gadsby, an Australian lesbian comedian, posted about the impact her state's campaign against legalizing homosexuality had on her in the 1990s. She said she learned that she "was subhuman during a debate where only the most horrible voices and ideas were amplified by the media." That we can still do this to young people twenty years later fills me with despair for our political process.

The plebiscite was blocked in the senate; conservatives threatened that the topic won't be addressed again by this government and we'll have to wait three more years, until our next election, before it can be reconsidered. It's so tedious, all this political strategizing: keeping party-room promises, angling to take credit for reform, landing blows on the other party. Even in the preparation for a possible plebiscite, the Australian media was full of opinion pieces about why our personal relationship should be held up to be the business of everybody. It's an astonishing hypocrisy to me that the opponents of same-sex marriage are often politically conservative; they are the very people who are opposed to government intervening in their lives, yet they think the government should intervene in ours.

At our friends' wedding, we saw that people had traveled, some from overseas, to be part of this ceremony, to witness the choice to stand publicly and declare, "We are committed to each other" and to have that commitment endorsed by the state. While we don't feel we need this endorsement, marriage would carry some practical considerations for my Dutch partner and me. She has a permanent resident visa in Australia, but can't have dual citizenship according to Dutch law—unless, that is, she is married to someone with another citizenship. For the most part there is no problem; she doesn't particularly need the dual citizenship. However, her permanent resident status here depends on her being in Australia for defined periods of time, and in her job, overseas posting is a real possibility, which might lead to her visa being revoked. But if we married, she could have dual citizenship without having to give up her birth nationality, and she wouldn't be worried about the travel conditions of her permanent resident visa.

There is also the peripheral endorsement that comes not just with a personal decision to marry or not, but with how society treats you if you are able to marry. Marriage equality would mean we'd be less fearful of how we talk about our domestic situation at work, less calculating in choosing who to say what to, when. It would mean the burden of carrying someone else's prejudice would shift back over that fence to their side.

It's one thing to experience the abstract political process that reveals other people's inability to see our loving, stable, happy relationship. It's another to be confronted by it much closer to home. We had left our friends' wedding feeling happy: happy for the couple, happy for having rekindled connections with their friends, happy for having been part of the collective goodwill and celebration. We were then brought back to earth pretty quickly when a close family member said to my partner, "Perhaps you'll meet someone in that new job you've got." We felt winded. Meet someone? She doesn't need a new someone. She has me. We have each other. We've been together for more than ten years. We've bought a house together, each of us has lost a parent while we've been together, we've lived in two countries together. We've been each other's rock for all of that time. In one fell swoop, this person revealed the depth of their blindness to our commitment. We've been sending love notes to each other and cooking meals and laughing at silly movies and sharing elated whoops at the top of mountains and mopping fevered brows, in sickness and in health; all of this is—in that person's world—nothing. What's even more annoying is that we *are* living the suburban domestic life that person wants us to live, except that we're both women. We go shopping on Saturday mornings. We grow vegetables in the backyard. I can't even imagine the social pressure on people whose relationships don't follow this model and are even more subject to social critique.

I'm looking for the kind of society that exists in most of my daily interactions and when I'm surrounded by friends, a society where I can actually forget for a while that there's anything about me worthy of the judgment of a nation. I'm looking for the kind of society where people like Elizabeth Gilbert don't have to ask the public for their "grace" while she's nursing her dying partner. I'm looking for a society that lets its government do important things, like stopping human rights abuses in refugee camps, instead of wasting all this time and money on an issue that can easily be changed with a stroke of a pen, as we saw when the *Marriage Act* was changed in 2004. As I write this in 2016, same-sex couples can marry in twenty-one countries. Australia, ostensibly so progressive, is way behind.

I hope that the outcome of all this politicking is that people see sense somehow and just pass the legislation. Despite all evidence to the contrary, I'm still hoping that perhaps Malcolm, our conservative Prime Minister, has made a secret deal with Bill Shorten, the Labor opposition leader, in a quiet bathroom stall somewhere.

"Hey, Bill?"

"Yes, Malcolm?"

"I don't want to do this. You know I don't want to do this. I'm a money man. There's a lot of money in gay weddings."

"I know. I'm a union man. You've got to see that I want unions—between organized labor, between people. I'm all about working together. Stick it to the bosses."

"So listen, Bill. You'll have to push back and keep pushing. I've just got to make those fascists think I'm going to keep working for the plebiscite, but you blocked it—so, I've done all I can, haven't I?"

"Yes, and you know it's obvious that I'm going to introduce my own change to the legislation, so that we can do what Howard did in 2004 and just sneak it through."

"It's going to be Christmas soon. How about you get that ready, and on the last day of sittings I'll make sure all the right-wingers are busy opening shopping centers or something and we'll pass it."

"Deal, Malcolm. I'm on it. And listen, when we get this through, I know people in all the relevant unions who can make sure you get that pink-dollar business."

Enough

BY VANESSA SHANTI FERNANDO

I.

I WASN'T EXPECTING THE BREAKUP, LET ALONE ALL THAT came after.

Writing about your relationship (as I did in *Dear John, I Love Jane*) takes supreme arrogance. It is a special sort of curse. The words in my original piece were so unapologetically hopeful, so wide open. "I am with the most amazing person in the world," I had written. I'm stunned that I had the nerve to think it, let alone write it down on paper.

And yet, we were perfect until we weren't. We met online—I in Canada, she in Mexico—so the very fact of us stumbling across each other's dating profiles felt like a minor kind of miracle. She used the word "quintessential" in her profile and it didn't hurt that she was gorgeous: masculine of center and boyish, an out lesbian in a border town. I sent her a message despite my cautious self, and when she wrote back I felt my stomach flip.

I fell in love with the idea of her before we met in person.

She wrote letters with her fountain pen and drew little cartoons in the margins. We whispered secrets over the phone like we were kids with tin cans pressed tight to our ears, attached with string. Two years passed like this, crammed full and urgent with plane trips, scrapbooks, late-night phone calls, and piles of letters.

By the time we found ourselves in the same city, it was clear that we were destined to be together. Fate was the only explanation that could make sense of the years we'd spent flirting and fantasizing over two thousand miles and two international borders. If there were other moments—when the space between us seemed to stretch thicker than geography—I didn't dwell on them. She had never been loved well by either parents or partners, so I told myself that I was the answer. I felt a swelling sense of pride and purpose when I thought about how I would now be able to fill in her hollow places with the strength of my longing for her, and the home we could start building together.

She was, all of a sudden, a daily fleshy constant. For our anniversary, she made me mac and cheese, putting candles on the table. We did our laundry together, mingling socks and underwear, and stored our Sarah Waters books on the same shelf. On weekends we went grocery shopping together. She liked anything processed, especially the snack packs of crackers with a tiny square of liquid orange cheese.

But she didn't like my friends. They were pretentious, she said. She was all about having the ability to take a joke, to not be too sensitive, to laugh at tragedy. She had seen a lot of tragedy, so I deferred to her on this, even though I felt uncomfortable sometimes with the jokes she chose to laugh at. At school and in the organizing collectives to which I belonged, we talked frequently about acknowledging our privilege. Deferring to her seemed like an extension of this practice. What I didn't allow myself to acknowledge was the doubt that unfurled in sticky tendrils, once in awhile, in the pit of my stomach.

And then a friend of mine died, right around the time that her parents disowned her for being a lesbian. I couldn't stop coughing, doubling over in fits on the bus, in class, in the movie theater. She played video games for hours. She didn't want me to touch her. We lay in bed night after night for months with our bodies curved away from one another like crescent moons from distant calendars.

One night, all that had been silent and swollen burst. She'd gone out drinking and come home wasted, loud, and messy. I'd had enough of her drinking. She'd had enough of my social-justice jargon, my not-so-silent disapproval. I cleaned her puke from around the toilet while she slept, slung diagonally across the bed. Afterward, I sat out in the hallway and cried—letting myself acknowledge, finally, that my love wasn't enough to fix this.

After all the noise—the packing, the plane ticket, the fighting, the ripping up of photos and scrapbooks, the hollow pledge to try and stay friends—after all that, the end was anticlimactic. I had spent many nights before she arrived imagining what it would be like to live together, finally. I'd close my eyes and picture the two of us lying together on my tiny bed. I'd zoom the frame out, seeing the apartment on Clark Street, with its narrow staircase and the zig-zagging streets of the Plateau Mont-Royal all around us. Now the picture faded, crumpled. After all that imagining, there was just me, the bedroom we'd shared, the remnants of a Montréal summer.

II.

I step off the bus and navigate Ontario Street until I reach the storefront I'm looking for. JJ's barbershop is tucked away on a side street, flanked by a cobbler on one end and a *dépanneur* on the other. There's an elaborate display of bow ties in the window, next to a small hand-painted sign saying "lesbian haircuts for everyone." I push open the door and see him sweeping up from his last cut. I've never met JJ, but I've heard his name over and over from cute queers with shaved undercuts. He's slight with wavy brown hair shaved at the side. He's wearing a button-up shirt that cuts close to his frame, slim pants, and oxford shoes. On someone else the look would read as conservative, but on him it looks sexy and just a little bit fey.

JJ nods at me and pats the chair. I sit down.

"What can I do for you today?" he asks. He spins the chair around so that I can see myself in the mirror, and talks to my reflection. My hair is thick and dark, the color of mud. It's growing out past my shoulders into a distinctly triangular shape.

"I want a lesbian haircut," I joke. What I mean is *define me. Make me recognizable. Help me be seen.*

"What does that mean?" he says, smiling. "Every haircut can be a lesbian haircut. That's the point."

I feel chastened. Called out. *I'm weak*, I want to tell him. *I just want the social approval that comes from conforming more closely to queer aesthetics, which are too often conflated with masculine-of-center presentations. In other words, I'm single and I want queers to ask me out on dates.*

"I was thinking something asymmetrical," I say.

We settle on half long, half short. I get a fringe and long curls down one side, and a shaved cut on the other. As soon as the hair starts falling, I feel a sense of relief. I check out my reflection in the mirror. I can't quite recognize myself. It feels good.

On my way home, I notice that my new hair is working its magic. I notice queers giving me the eye far more than usual. I feel cute, so I practice flirting. My preferred method involves holding the person's gaze for a beat longer than usual, smirking just a little, and then looking away. It's a nice day to practice. Hot and bright, but not sticky.

I've already got a date lined up for tonight. I'll be meeting up with Laura, a green-haired zinester I met on the same website as my ex. Our compatibility rating is 90 percent, so I had to message her. Her photos are full riot grrrl. She's wearing ripped baby-doll dresses and smeared eyeliner, and she has full tattoo sleeves.

I wear a new shirt. It's a collared short-sleeved button up, pastel yellow with faded pink sleeves that reminds me of melting Neapolitan ice cream. I button the shirt up all the way, even though it feels tight around my neck. It's important to button the shirt right to the top to get the look right: it's the difference between cute androgynous queer and feminine business casual. This summer I'm learning that *hot* means *androgynous* means *far away from femme*, unless you're going for dandy. I've stowed my summer dresses at the back of my closet, and donated most of the clothes that my ex liked me to wear (the strappy tank tops, the high-heeled shoes, the lingerie). I feel lucky to be lanky and flat-chested. It makes it easier for me to conform.

I wait for Laura outside of Aux Vivres, a popular vegan joint near my apartment. I'm not sure what to do with my hands. I cross and uncross my arms. I try leaning against the wall of the restaurant, but it feels too forced. I resort to taking my phone out of my pocket and scanning old e-mail messages, just to have something to do.

Finally, I see Laura walking towards me. I recognize her immediately; she looks just like her pictures. She's wearing a pink-and-purple striped tube top, cut-off denim shorts over black fishnet stockings, and scruffy combat boots. Her hair is long, straight, and algae green.

We smile at each other. I give her an awkward wave and tell her it's really nice to meet her in person. "Do you do hugs?" she asks me. I nod, and she pulls me close.

The hug is brief and businesslike. "Should we go inside?" she says. I nod again. *So far so good.*

They seat us in the center of the room. Servers swerve around us, carrying trays piled high with rice bowls, chickpea wraps, and carob-date shakes. She tells me she's studying to become a librarian. She rests her arm on the table and shows me the tattoo on her inner arm: a stack of thick books, each one with a different colored cover. She's always loved writing, and she started self-publishing her poems in photocopied chapbooks when she was eleven. She sold them to her parents, her teachers, her friends at school. I tell her about my history classes and about the book I'm reading (Zoe Whittall's *Holding Still for as Long as Possible*). I tell her about my cat, who hisses every time anyone but me comes near her. And I tell her that this is my first date in a very long while. Soon the space between us feels calm and loose. We're making eye contact across the table. I forget about my flirting technique. I'm not smirking, not looking away.

We both order the BLT sandwich, made with smoked coconut flakes instead of bacon, and vegan mayonnaise. "I like your hair," she says. "I've been thinking about cutting mine."

"Thanks. I just felt like a change. But yours is awesome. I love the color."

She shrugs. "It's always a different color. I can't even remember what color it is naturally anymore."

"When did you first start dyeing it?"

"Oh, ages ago. Probably when I first started dating my boyfriend. He always hated it when I dyed my hair, so that made me want to do it more."

"You have a boyfriend?"

"Ex-boyfriend," Laura corrected herself. "We just broke up."

"I'm sorry to hear that," I said.

"I'm not. It should have happened a long time ago."

"So why did it end now?"

Laura looked at me and smirked. "I was totally in love with

my best friend for a long time, but I was in denial about it. I don't know what happened—one day I just couldn't shrug it off anymore. So I told him. I don't know what I was expecting."

"How did he take it?"

"He was kind of into it, actually. I think he wanted us to have a threesome or something. And that just felt really gross to me. And then I realized I actually just wanted to sleep with my friend. I didn't want him to have anything to do with it." She laughed. She had a great laugh—big and loud and not at all self-conscious. It made me laugh too.

"So why aren't you with your friend tonight?" I ask.

Laura shook her head. "No dice."

"She wasn't into it?"

"Not even in the slightest."

"Lucky me," I say.

We look at each other. I smile. I can feel a new quality taking shape inside me: something bold and strong and confident. Laura's blushing. She looks at me like she's seeing me for the first time. It's that look you get when your own capacity for desire surprises you. I remember the feeling.

III.

"You keep talking about the ways you'd like to grow and change," my therapist says. "But what if the person you are now is actually enough, just as you are? How would that feel?" She is leaning back in her leather chair, a red shawl wrapped around her shoulders. I feel that familiar quiver in the base of my throat, that painful, low thrum.

I shake my head. "I don't know what that means," I tell her. It hurts when I talk. My throat feels hot and tight.

"I see some emotion there," she tells me.

Screw you, I think. *No you don't.* I can feel the tears in the corner of my eyes. I nod. "Typical overachiever," I say. I think I've kept my voice mostly steady, in control.

"How would it be to allow yourself to feel that emotion?" she asks me. When she's slipping into her therapist mode, her voice gets low and smooth as her scarf. It seems cliché, but it works, too. I nod, resigned. I close my eyes. The Feeling wells up. It's right in the center of my chest. It's building, the edges crackling with energy. The tears come.

"When you think about being enough, what happens?" she asks me. "Picture it."

My eyes are closed. I picture it. I see a figure letting its arms down, and I feel lightness release. "I picture arms coming down, releasing. And I see this golden-yellow color," I tell her. "But I don't trust it."

She nods. "Of course you don't trust it," she says. "It's unfamiliar."

I breathe in deep, then exhale. My shoulders move down. "Yeah," I say. "I don't know what it would mean, or what it would change."

"That makes sense," she says. "You don't know if it's a friend. But I wonder, how would it feel to invite that yellow color a little bit closer?"

The hour goes by so quickly. When I walk outside it's noon, and the sun is bright and hot. It's been a warm, dry summer in Vancouver. I moved out west two years ago for grad school, after I decided that I wanted to become a social worker.

Leaving the session feels disorienting—I still feel like there's a small tight ball in the center of my chest. I walk along Broadway for two blocks in the wrong direction before I notice and retrace my steps. When I finally get to Heartwood Cafe, nestled next to a Starbucks at Broadway and Kingsway, the tightness in my chest is gone but my stomach is churning.

Heartwood Cafe is huge, with bright walls covered in artwork.

The featured artists rotate regularly. This month, there are framed black-and-white photographs of people who identify as butch. I do a quick scan of the space, taking in two staff members chatting behind the counter, a busy room echoing with a friendly buzz of voices, a toddler playing with a toy kitchenette in the corner. I see Carmen by the window. I recognize her from her Facebook profile, although we've never met. She's tall and thin with short, curly hair. She's sitting alone at a large table, drinking coffee, and looking at her phone. Her nails, curved around the white mug, are long and painted. I hesitate at the entrance of Heartwood.

She looks up and sees me. Smiles and waves. I approach. Introductions. She compliments my necklace—a strand of moonstone, with a black tourmaline pendant in the center. The moonstone is for dreaming; the tourmaline is for protection. I sit down and order coffee with sugar and cream.

We talk about astrology. Carmen is a Virgo, though she isn't sure how much she believes in that. She loves cats, but she doesn't have one of her own. She works in human resources; she's also a painter. She talks quickly, smiles often. The knot in my stomach starts to relax.

Soon the others start to arrive. Amber is wearing a bright-patterned dress and purple lipstick. Eva has an infectious smile and knees scuffed from roller derby. Rae, with the blue hair, is coming straight from a pottery class and has grey streaks all over her forearms. We introduce ourselves. We name our connections—the way we each came to find out about mixie brunch. It's a new tradition—a monthly brunch meetup for queers who identify as mixed race.

"I'm so glad this exists," Eva says, as she pulls her sweater over her head and drapes it on the back of her chair. "This city is so white, it's ridiculous."

We go around the table, naming our own and our ancestors'

stories of migration. We talk about colonialism, diaspora, and our complicity as settlers on stolen Coast Salish land. Some of us have a white parent and some of us don't. Some of us identify as femme and some of us don't. Some of us are cis and some of us aren't. All of us are queer, and we are many other things, too: parents, survivors, artists.

We order eggs and toast and coffee, and we take our time. We talk about dismantling white supremacy; moisturizing dark, curly hair; combating anti-blackness; the best sushi places. We share perspectives around transformative justice responses to sexual assault, debrief Eva's frustrating experiences at work, and laugh at Rae's stories about their disastrous Tinder dates. We hold a lot back from each other, too. We're shy. We swap glances then look away. We are all hurting in our own ways. We have all loved before, and we've been left all the worse and all the better for it.

"It feels amazing to be sitting here together," Carmen says. There are nods around the table. It's true; I can feel our collective energy as we share a meal, beautifully queer in our brown and black skin. I watch their faces: listening, laughing, sipping coffee. I feel recognition flicker through me. This is what I have been looking for. I feel steady. I feel seen.

I sit back for a moment, listening as Carmen and Amber banter back and forth about the process of going scent-free. Just for a moment, I let myself picture that golden-yellow color close around me. I take a breath, imagining flecks of gold traveling down into my lungs and nestling deep into my belly. While I can still feel the knot in my stomach, when I exhale, I can feel it loosen. Just for a moment I think, *maybe this is enough.* And then the moment passes. Eva stretches, her crop top riding up her ribcage. I cradle my coffee mug between both hands, enjoying the warmth.

Kama Sutra

BY KRISTA FRETWELL

THERE IS NO INSTRUCTION MANUAL FOR WHAT WE DO.

I recently changed the wax seal under our bathroom toilet, wrench in hand, down on my knees, cheek-by-jowl with my lover's ex-husband. I live in the house where he and my partner were once married. The bedroom they shared, the bed where she and I now sleep, is a few feet over from where we were sloshing water out of the toilet tank, trying to get it repositioned over a drain hole in the floor. My partner's ex-husband is our landlord now, and he is a friend.

There is no road map for how to get from there to here.

Here's the thing about repression—it usually isn't conscious. Typically, the thing that we can't admit, or don't want to know, or can't allow to be true about ourselves, gets subverted and buried before it ever fully enters into our awareness. It is a kind of willful ignorance, symptomatic of our judging minds. I accept responsibility for not being aware that I was in deep danger of falling in love with a woman—with someone else's wife. We were only planning to go out for tea. When I told my husband that some-thing was happening and I wanted permission to see what it was, what I didn't know that I meant was I had just fallen in love with someone and was wondering if he would mind if I poured gaso-line all over the fire.

If there is a thread that weaves all of this together, it is flying by the seat of our pants.

We were in love before we even knew what had hit us. There was no time to research; it never occurred to us to read about what we were supposed to do next. What came next, came next. natu-rally. First, her hand touched my hand, and there was a power surge all the way into the next county. We both knew that some-thing terrible and wonderful had happened. Once we kissed, it was enough to know that it would never be enough. We were unwittingly, yet willingly, in a state of foreplay that lasted for weeks; between stolen meetings of our hearts in school rooms and libraries and sad kitchens, where we had been so lonely without each other just a few weeks before. Neither of us had ever been with another woman. When we finally gave ourselves over completely to each other, I felt like a fish that had been thrown back into water. We didn't need anyone to show us what to do.

If there are directions for how this is done, we are making them up as we go.

Did you know that sexual positions make up only a small portion of the *Kama Sutra*? The rest of it consists of aphorisms on the art of living a pleasurable, yet virtuous, life. I have always thought that my sexual awakening was merely a microcosm of awakening to life itself. Denial, for me, meant living my life with one arm tied behind my back. I have come to realize that the more at home

I am in my own body, the more at home I am in the world. I feel how, when my lover and I are together sexually—giving and receiving, ebbing and flowing, responding to each other's subtle or urgent gestures, trading power, exchanging energy—we are simply practicing for everything else that we do together every day. Much in the same way that, when children play, they are doing the deep work that prepares them for how they will grow— we just have to get out of their way. We have to get out of our own way.

I wanted to live a life of integrity, so I recollected all the missing pieces of myself.

Listening to your heart and following your desire will not always bring pleasure. Nothing could have prepared me for breaking my best friend's heart. It brought me no pleasure to watch him kick an anguished hole into our bedroom door, or to hold him like he was a wounded animal while he railed and howled against impending loss. Nothing could have steadied me for my own grief—for the rivers upon oceans of tears, seemingly without end—still streaming now as I write this. Nothing could have trained me to stand and listen while my lover's husband yelled that I was ruining his life, as we were unpacking our trunks at the school picnic. No one taught me how to know—even in the midst of this storm, when everyone I loved and everything I'd ever learned was telling me I was wrong— that I was right. No one had ever shown me how to trust myself, so I learned it the hard way—by doing it.

Here's an aphorism: No one else can instruct you how to be your one and only wise and true self.

The man that I married is one of the most beautiful souls I have ever known. After months of wrestling with the question of what to do about our marriage—both of us worn thin from the anxiety and grief—we finally decided to divorce. He wanted to stay married, but only if things could go back to the way that they were—me, not gay—which they couldn't. So, he told me that he wanted to let me go like water: soft and gentle, not clinging, but flowing in the direction of gravity. We bought new rings, which we now wear on our right hands, as a sign of our continued commitment to each other in love, friendship, and parenting our children. We went to our favorite spot, on a flat, gray rock overlooking the river, and exchanged our love stories for each other. Then we stripped ourselves naked, held hands, and plunged into the cold, dark water, together as one for the last time.

Love is a river that never ends. It cuts deep into the soft earth of us, forging new channels as it flows.

Grief, like love, lives in the body. It is a mysterious, amorphous entity that does not observe the laws of time and space, or obey our wishes to be rid of it. Grief for the loss of my best friend—my partner in marriage for fifteen years—took me to my knees. There were moments that I literally could not stand. A simple walk in the woods to clear my head would bring me back around to my flayed-open heart; I'd find myself face down in the dirt, sobbing, my body leaden with sadness, unable to take another step.

Love is a choice. Love is not a choice. Our loving hearts are infinitely more rich and complex than what we conceive of when we say "choose."

A few days ago, my seventy-one-year-old mother quietly pulled up a chair across the kitchen table from where I was sitting, her gentle face quivering in an attempt to choke back tears. "I am sorry that I didn't know what you were going through when you were younger, and that I didn't help you," she said. My mother has always been an example for me of parental humility. When I was a child, she came to me like this when her conscience was haunting her about something, and would confess that she was sorry for speaking harshly or for making a mistake in judgment. My parents did the best that they could with what they had—both of them were raised, and together brought up their children, in conservative Christian churches that abhorred homosexuality. When I came out to my parents six years ago, they gave me a gift that continues to unfold for all of us—they showed up. They set aside their fear—for me, and for my husband and our children, whom they love—they put down the rule book and they accepted, and above all *trusted*, me. The best that they could do got even better, because they found the courage to love from the very ground of not knowing.

The only sanctification that I ever needed was this: love's kiss.

It hasn't been a straight or easy path. When romantic relationships fall apart there is anger and hurt and jealousy—even rage. For us, what began as utter devastation has taken years and a deliberate vision to sort through—with patience, humility, cooperation, generosity, the courage to show up for each other no matter how painful or difficult—added together with the incredibly good fortune that we all genuinely enjoy and respect one another as human beings. We didn't quit our marriages for lack of fondness. These days, we all look out for one another. My partner, our children, and their fathers—we share holidays and birthdays, swap cars, lend tools or a helping hand. We've hiked and skied and run 5K races together. Our children know that they are loved and supported by adults who care about each other and want what is best for everyone. When my father was gravely ill in the hospital last year, my partner's ex-husband sent him flowers. Last spring, my partner, my ex-husband, and I climbed to the eight-thousand-foot summit of Mt. St. Helens alongside our twelve-year-old daughter. These are our triumphs. These are our blessings. It is becoming increasingly difficult to tell them apart.

There is a thread that, when pulled, is tied to everything else.

There is no magic formula for whom to love or how to have sex or what to do with heartbreak. There is no one right way to welcome joy and grief when they arrive on your doorstep at the same time. There is no road map for how to come out as gay when you are married to a man and have children—for how to let go of *what was* with dignity and grace, while still holding steady and fast to every last ounce of the love that is still shared; for how to be present with and accept the humanity of anger and jealousy and the deep pain of loss; for how to navigate the logistics of divorce and multiple households, complex emotions, new joys and pains amidst the old; for when and how to forge ahead and blend a new family, and raise a new tribe out of the ashes of the past. Five children, three households, two ex-husbands, their new girlfriends, good friends who have stood by us all along the way. We're making it up as we go. We're learning to do this by heart. Every day we begin again—everything else is just details.

White Horse Optional

BY G. LEV BAUMEL

I CAN TOUCH BOTH WALLS OF THE AIRPLANE BATHROOM
with my elbows. Turning around takes some negotiation. It smells
like flowery air freshener and the many people who have been in
here before me. A soggy strip of toilet paper is stuck to the floor.
I feel something wet in my underwear and check the lock before
pulling down my pants where, for the first time, I find a small
puddle of blood. I am twelve years old.

My mother is not with us. My parents have recently split up
and my younger brother and I are flying to Argentina with my
father to visit my great-grandmother on her ninetieth birthday.
Had my mother been there, I probably would still have turned
to him. He was the one I trusted; he always knew what to do.
He shrugged, "What do you want me to do about it?" before
returning to his magazine.

Until that moment, it was easy to maneuver between genders.
I actively refused to wear anything pink or frilly; I wore my hair
in a spiky crew cut. Weekends were spent handing my father
hammers and screwdrivers as we tackled the endless projects in the

turn-of-the-century house he bought when I was eight. Together, we cleaned out gutters, chopped through decades of weeds, rewired. I carried twenty-five-pound bags of dirt and scrubbed the hubcaps of his Jaguar E-type, which I referred to as the favorite child, with a toothbrush.

I remember telling my mother I wanted to be just like him. He was confident and driven, he could sand down walls, he won every negotiation, he put together Ikea furniture without the instructions. My father waited for no one and asked no one for permission. To me, he was the strongest man in the world. My mother, on the other hand, did her best to be invisible. She asked if she could maybe possibly go to the bathroom. A decision as small as what to make for dinner was agonizing.

Rarely did the word "woman" come out of my father's mouth without "stupid," "idiotic" or "fucking" attached. Women were untrustworthy, intent on stealing his money. Women were governed by emotion—a four-letter word in our house; they were all terrible drivers and shouldn't be allowed on the road. As far as I could tell, there were no redeeming qualities to being a woman.

I hadn't ever connected my father's opinions about women to my being one. But in the time it took us to fly to the Southern hemisphere, I went from being his sidekick to becoming "one of them." Softness, femininity, anything that could be perceived as weakness was the enemy.

When we returned from Buenos Aires, Joseph, a neighbor and my father's best friend, came to pick us up. Joseph burst through the security line and flung himself into my father's arms. My father laughed uncomfortably. "Whoa," he said, backing up slightly. A few months later, I discovered they were lovers.

When the secret came out at school, kids whispered and stared. "Your dad's a fag," they laughed.

School was hard, but home was harder. I tried, and failed, to engage my dad. I would have done anything to get him to love me again. Instead, he openly preferred my brother Paul, because he was a boy.

"Guess what happened this morning?" I bounded into his office during my seventh-grade lunch break. "The math teacher—"

My father sighed loudly but didn't look up from his desk. "Don't you ever shut up?"

Deflated, I skulked to the kitchen to soothe myself with whatever I could find in the fridge.

It didn't help that my body had its own agenda. Although I did my best to hide my breasts under baggy T-shirts, they were unmistakable. My body was all roundness. I could not pass as a boy anymore—and even if I had wanted to be a traditional, diminutive woman, it was clear that I was not built to be one.

At school, instead of being quiet and unobtrusive, as I understood women should be, I did my best to be assertive and voice my opinions aggressively, to come across as more masculine. I became a loud know-it-all. "Fuck you," featured heavily in my lexicon.

"Don't fucking swear," my father slapped me across the face when he heard me curse.

Because I was more like him, I wondered whether my father's orientation would pass on to me. The first time someone accused me of being a lesbian, I had to look the word up. I declared that I was attracted to people, not genders, an answer crafted both in self-defense as well as to remain loyal to my father. It made little sense: I hated being a woman, why would I want to be *with* one? Still, the question lodged itself in my mind like a sailor's knot.

There was nobody to ask. I started exploring new parts of myself. I grew my hair out, attempted dresses and makeup. In the beginning, being a girl felt more like a Halloween costume than a part of me.

To add to my confusion, I didn't lack for male attention outside my home. Sex became my way of engaging. Their socks on the floor, the sound of their skin against the sheets, the smell of their sweat. I focused on details to keep the big picture blurry, hovering a safe distance above my life as if watching it on a screen. Emotion, still a dirty word, was to be avoided at all costs.

"You're all woman," my lovers told me. I smiled at the irony. Being "all woman" was what I longed for. Secretly, I also still wanted to go back to being the little boy my father had once loved. By then, he had chosen to disappear from my life altogether. He didn't want a daughter—the only thing I could be.

The schism inside me was deep, unbridgeable. When a man told me he loved me, first, anxiety would set in; then, I would go numb. I left before he could.

I was twenty-three when I met Cathy. Eight years older, she was everything I wasn't: bold, fearless, comfortable in her skin. Cathy straddled her masculine and feminine gracefully, pulling on her heavy cowboy boots and fastening her large silver belt buckles with perfectly manicured fingers. She was meticulous about her long, blond hair. The rings on her fingers were chunky, mostly skulls.

I had never met a woman like her. When she was sad, she cried. When she was angry, she ranted. When she was happy, she allowed herself to be. To me, Cathy's strength was masculine, her vulnerability, deeply feminine. She inspired me and terrified me. I was attracted to her—and her desire for me was intoxicating.

But the difference wasn't only in her. With Cathy, I didn't feel I had to pretend to be anyone else. I allowed myself to delve into my feminine and masculine sides, my fears, my tears.

Most nights after work, Cathy and I would meet at the bar where the woman she had a crush on waitressed. It wasn't a pretty place and the carpet smelled like stale beer. But the guacamole was fantastic and the object of Cathy's desires snuck us free drinks despite not reciprocating Cathy's feelings.

From the beginning, people assumed we were a couple. I was aware that all it would take was encouragement on my part. Neither of us said a word and nothing happened. Instead, I remained in the never-ending push-me-pull-me cycle of commitmentphobia. I launched myself into every new relationship hoping this man would be "the one," only to flee as soon as things threatened to become serious.

With Cathy, I was home. Still, it was men whose beds I coveted.

Enter Ethan. He was reliable, he'd had the same friends since college, he was a regular guy whom I could trust to never stop loving me. In hindsight, I chose to marry Ethan because Ethan chose me.

On my wedding day, I fantasized about calling my father. "See, someone loves me!" I would tell him. He was not at my wedding. That doesn't mean I didn't feel his presence as strongly as if he'd been standing behind me telling me I looked ridiculous in my wedding dress.

Cathy joined Ethan and me for drinks at a bar in downtown Manhattan when we signed our official wedding papers. Lying naked together, years later, she teased me about what I told her in the ladies' room that night: "Nothing can happen between us. I'm married now." I was too drunk to remember that conversation, although I do remember how happy I was to have her there.

By then, Cathy and I had drifted apart. We rarely saw each other in person but kept abreast of the broad strokes of each other's lives through social media.

I thought marrying Ethan would fill the empty part of me where my father's love had once brimmed. Four years and one child in, however, my anchor had become my noose.

Wrapped up in the latest must-have stroller and the search for the kindergarten that would guarantee my child entry to Yale, I had become the kind of person Cathy and I made fun of.

At dinner, Ethan and I sat on either side of our daughter. At night, she slept between us. Our exchanges were brief and perfunctory. Every interaction was a minefield of passive aggression; even a request to pick up milk held the potential for an explosion.

I reverted to disengaging from my life, watching it from a distance, as I had in the past, only this time, I had committed to this movie until death do us part. "I know I must love you," I told Ethan, "I just can't feel a thing."

The emotional dirty laundry piled up. I started to suffer from dizzy spells. I went from doctor to doctor in a quest to figure out what was wrong, spent hundreds of dollars on herbs and pills and potions. I signed up for cleanses and detoxes. For a while, I got better. Better never lasted.

Ethan and I attempted therapy but ultimately agreed that we spent more time talking about how to fix the relationship than being in it.

Our two-year-old daughter said, "Mamma crying again."

When she was born, I had promised myself I would offer her a better example than what I'd had as a child. Something had to change.

"What is it you want?" Ethan asked.

I had no answer.

Then I dreamed of Cathy every night for two weeks. It had been a few years since we'd spoken. She had moved to Philadelphia.

"Can I come see you?" I asked, too nervous to say anything else.

She laughed as if my question was a silly one.

A week later, Cathy was waiting when my train pulled into the station. I saw her first and smiled for what felt like the first time in months. She hugged me tight. I dug my face into her neck, inhaling the scent that is hers alone. Being near her brought tears to my eyes. While the scene could easily have been in a movie, Cathy felt very, very real. Unlike in the rest of my life, I was right there with my feet on the ground, feeling my arms around her, and hers around me.

She carried my bag to her car and held the door for me. We caught up on the drive back to her place: I'd had a child, she'd been in her usual plethora of messy entanglements. She'd traveled around the world, I'd moved continents a couple of times. She asked about Ethan.

"My life has become like an itchy wool sweater that's shrunk in the wash," I admitted. "No matter how hard I wrestle to fit into it, it's too uncomfortable."

Cathy had watched many of her friends go through divorce. She was sympathetic but pragmatic. "You'll get through it, and you'll move on."

Cathy winked at me. She didn't know this time was different. "Let me give you a tour," she said when we arrived at her cottage.

I nodded, restraining myself from kissing her. The house was tiny, the walls and surfaces filled with mementos and photographs from Cathy's adventures: snapshots with friends, artwork. She loved turquoise. Every piece had a story. The rug under my feet was thick and soft. "Tea?" she asked.

When we got to the kitchen, I pulled her to me. I kissed her, my hands reaching under her shirt. I wanted to feel every bit of her, which I did, later that night under the Christmas tree.

Returning to the apartment Ethan and I still shared at the end of the weekend was nearly impossible. I reminded myself that I was a mother first and foremost—I no longer had the luxury of fleeing. I turned the key in the lock, pushed the door open, and confessed to my husband as quickly as I could.

Surprisingly, after my revelation about Cathy, Ethan quieted down. The way he saw it, if I was into women, there was nothing he could do. He also absolved me: it wasn't my fault I was a lesbian, it was nature. In his mind, it was simple.

Not so for me.

Loving Cathy was both the strangest and the most natural thing in the world. I knew her so well, yet everything about her was suddenly new. When she came to New York for a few days, she booked herself into a hotel in the Meatpacking District. The room was expensive and sparse. Cathy's designer jeans and well-worn boots stood out against the minimalist decor. I pressed her against the floor-to-ceiling window overlooking the Highline. With Cathy, I was in charge. Afterwards, we got into a deep bath together, giggling at how pretty the square tub was — and how uncomfortable. "It has no curves," I complained.

We explored the city as we had throughout our friendship. The difference was that now, instead of sharing lunch, we held hands and kissed.

Cathy came to my apartment with Ethan's blessing while he was at work. She noticed that some of the light bulbs in the living room were burned out. With a matter-of-factness I found irresistible, Cathy climbed the stepladder and switched out the dead bulbs for working ones.

When Ethan came home later that day, he noticed the room was brighter. "What happened?" he asked, looking at the ceiling.

"Cathy changed the light bulbs."

"Well, if that doesn't kill the last shreds of my masculinity," he said.

As my marriage was ending, so too were the dreams I'd had about what I thought I wanted. I thought Ethan could save me from the wreckage of my childhood. Then, I pinned my hopes on Cathy to save me from my marriage. It mattered little whether it was Prince or Princess Charming—what I needed was to be saved (white horse optional).

Of course that wasn't going to happen. Walking the five

blocks from the subway to my apartment, passing the hodge-podge of old-world brownstones and modern construction sites, I went from exhilaration to anxiety, from despair to anticipation. My commitment to my child was the only thing that didn't waver. She was, and remains, my compass. Still, everything was coated in a layer of guilt: blowing up my life was one thing, but was I wrecking my daughter's?

Ethan wanted to tell the world about his lesbian wife. He was intent on clearing himself of all responsibility in the demise of our marriage. Text messages started pouring in: *I'm envious of your ability to be true to yourself,* one friend wrote. *I wish I had your courage,* someone texted. I didn't know who or what I was, only that the label, *lesbian,* gave me the same shrunken, itchy sweater feeling as the label *wife.*

Loving Cathy became my panacea. Taking solace in her, I cautiously ventured out of my need to conform, reverting to my adolescent explorations. This time I reached way beyond femininity. What I was looking to do was get past any definition of gay or straight, female or male. I experimented with different clothing styles, got a new tattoo, and splurged on a pair of delicate gold earrings. I wore the long skirts I had once coveted and regretted having gotten rid of my Doc Martens for the first time in years. I was as scared as I was liberated.

I feared I was losing my mind. It wasn't that I didn't want to be with Cathy; I wasn't capable of being with anyone. As easily as my heart had flown open to embrace her, it slammed shut. "I need to figure out *me* before I can figure out *we,*" I tried to explain. She didn't buy it.

We agreed to stay friends. Cathy did her best, replying to my texts and taking my calls. She was understandably angry. I was broken; I was relieved. I longed to see her and was grateful for the train ride that separated us. After a while, we reverted to "liking" each other's pictures and posts on social media.

Ethan and I slowly separated. We moved to California and worked on building a healthy co-parenting friendship. I have yet to make peace with the fact that my father is out in the world choosing to pretend I don't exist—though his absence has served to make Ethan's gifts as a kind, devoted dad to our daughter all the more clear.

For a while, the breakup, the move, and being a mom were more than enough. When I thought about dating, the question that had sat in the back of my mind since age twelve was overwhelming: if I was to enter into a relationship, would I want it to be with a man or a woman?

One day, at the health-food store, I met a man. He was soft-spoken with long hair. He wore sandals and socks. I missed Cathy. She and I would have shared a laugh about the chakra and energy talk Californians seem obsessed with.

"But you're a lesbian!" Ethan exclaimed when I told him about the man.

I reminded him that he had been the one to make that decision.

"The only thing I am is confused," I said.

"So am I," he admitted.

The relationship with the man didn't last.

I joined a dating site. When given the option, I ticked the two boxes, indicating that I was open to meeting both men and women. I developed a crush on a woman but didn't have the guts to tell her. I fell in love again. This time with a man.

"You're all woman," he said one day after making love.

I smiled. "I feel it."

A few months ago, a white-haired stranger walked up to me and my daughter at the playground. The woman was dressed in blue silk. Even her glasses were blue. She bent down and asked my daughter: "Do you want to be a princess when you grow up?"

My child stared back at the woman. "I want to be a paleontologist astronaut. And a wildlife photographer."

The woman raised her eyebrows with a smile. Her eyes fell on me. "You are the person you've been looking for," she waved her hands in my face. "You are your own savior."

"I love you," the woman cried out doing a shuffle-dance, "I love everyone!"

My daughter and I giggled.

My daughter wants to know if she can marry a woman or a man when she grows up. I tell her she can marry whomever she wants. In fact, I specify, she can choose not to get married at all.

I'm grateful that my daughter isn't interested in princes and princesses.

This year, she's learning to ride a horse.

Whatever Happened?

BY ELIZABETH J. GERARD

Now

I HAVE TO CONFESS, I HAVE AN AGENDA, I HAVE A QUESTION . . .

She is famous. A famous movie star. Famous for her red-ringleted hair. Famous for her twenty-five-million-dollars-a-film salary. Famous for her glittering smile and tabloid-cover fodder. I am not famous.

I am of the hard-hit, lost job/money/house/husband, living in the latest of a long list of cheap apartments sort. She is a famous movie star and I think she knows what I need to know, so I wrangle my way into being her driver for the week. I will drive to O'Hare and pick her up. Drive her to the Drake Hotel. Drive her to the film sets. Drive her back to O'Hare. She is a famous movie star and I know that she knows, at least think she knows, what I need to know.

brick wall, she said everything was too much for her, too much. The last time I saw her, she said, *Peace Out,* then she disappeared.

Did she move? Maybe she moved.
Is she dead? Maybe she's dead.
(Please, God, don't let her be dead.)

Now

This might seem rude, I'm sorry if this seems rude, I don't mean to be rude . . .

God! How long has it been since I got really dressed up? So many moves. Always moving, moving, moving. A divorce then too many moves. A suicide attempt and a divorce and then I am constantly moving. I never settle, never unpack, never know where anything is. Where the fuck is my makeup/jewelry/skirts? A divorce will do that to you. A divorce after a suicide attempt will do that to you. You will lose everything.

A Lifetime Ago

My heart burst the first time I ever saw her. She, auditioning for a commercial in L.A. Me, producing that commercial in L.A. She stepped in front of the camera, so shy, so shy. Then she lifted her head, her eyes like golden topaz, her skin like Ethiopian soil, and she smiled. She just stepped in front of the camera, lifted her head, and smiled, and I knew, I knew, I knew she'd be in that commercial if I had to kill for her to be in it. If I had to kill. I knew she'd be in the commercial if I had to kill.

And now she is in the commercial. And now she's here at the wardrobe fitting. And now there's a box of wigs on the table. A box of wigs to cover her beautiful long black locks.

The white director doesn't like her long black locks. The white director wants to cover her long black locks. The white director says her long black locks make her look "too black."

She's so shy, but that smile. That smile! What can I do to make her smile? I pick a huge afro out of the box of wigs. I put the huge afro on my head. The afro covers my straight blonde hair. The afro covers my straight blonde hair that no one says makes me look "too white." I put the afro on and when she turns around I'm behind the table with the ridiculous afro on my head and she laughs so hard she doubles over and we both know, we both know. We're both laughing and catching the light in each other's eyes and the spark is there. The spark is there and we both know. But I am married. Back in Chicago my husband awaits my return from L.A. I am married and I love my husband awaiting my return. I love him. But she and I both know. She and I both know the spark is there but it won't go anywhere. It can't. Because what can be done, when there is nothing to be done?

Back Then

I tried to kill myself. I tell her everything while the sun slides behind the Santa Monica hotel room window and the room goes black. Lying fully clothed on our backs on the cheap orange bedspread like the dead in the dark, I tell her everything about my husband leaving me after I'd confessed my love for her to him. I tell her about wanting to die after my husband left me. I tell her how much I wanted to die that I downed a sixty-four-ounce bottle of vodka and all the meds I could find in my house. I tell her I actually did die. About being D.O.A. About the EMTs reviving me. About waking up in the hospital and wanting to die all over again.

I tell her that the years since we last saw each other, on the set in L.A., a wig covering her beautiful long black locks, have not been good to me. The years have not been good to me. *I'm going blind.* She tells me everything about the tumor that is blinding her. About the tumor that might kill her. She tells me about living out of her car after the red-ringleted, twenty-five-million-dollar-salary-glittering-smile,-tabloid-fodder-famous movie star told her she had to leave the guest house she'd been renting from her. That the famous movie star's white boyfriend didn't like a black lesbian renting the guest house. And so the famous white movie star told the black lesbian she had to go. She didn't care where.

(The famous movie star's white boyfriend didn't like a black lesbian renting the guest house. The famous movie star's white boyfriend told her she had to choose between him and the black lesbian. The famous movie star's white boyfriend told her the black lesbian had to go. So the famous movie star told the black lesbian she had to go. She didn't care where.)

She tells me that the years since we last saw each other, on the set in L.A., a wig covering her beautiful long black locks, have not been good to her. The years have not been good to her.

Lying on our backs fully clothed on the cheap orange bedspread in the tiny, dark Santa Monica hotel room with the window that looked out on a brick wall, we tell each other about everything that has happened to us since we last saw each other. We tell each other everything. Then for a long time we don't say anything. For a long time, we just listen to the sounds of our breaths drifting out into the dark, dark room.

But then—*then* she reached for my hand and just held it, her long black fingers wrapped around my small white ones. And then—*then* we turned to each other and kissed. And then—*then* we just held each other. And then—*then* we both cried. We held each other and cried for each other until we both fell asleep, fully clothed, on top of the cheap orange bedspread in the tiny dark Santa Monica hotel room with the window that looked out on a brick wall.

Now

I don't know if you know, but if you do know then I have to know because . . .

Because I loved her as soon as she stepped in front of that camera so, so many years ago. Because I've searched and searched and searched and after all these years I still can't find her. Because *Peace Out* was the last thing she said to me. The last thing she said after she took my hand, after we held each other all night long, after we wept for each other. Because she said *Peace Out,* then she disappeared.

(If she's dead, then she's dead. At least I know. It's the not knowing that's killing me.)

Back Then

After we woke in the morning in the tiny, dark Santa Monica hotel room with the window that looked out on a brick wall. After I said I had a plane to catch. After she said she had to go to work. After she hugged me so tightly. So, so tightly. Like she didn't want to let go. But then she did. She did let go. She let go, and after she let go, she said the last thing she ever said to me.

Peace Out.

Then she disappeared.

So. . . .

Now

I hate to ask but I have to ask because I think you might know, and it's been so many years since I first fell in love with her when I cast her in the commercial I was producing, and so many more years since I last saw her in that tiny, dark Santa Monica hotel room with the window that looked out on a brick wall, and she said she was going blind, and she said she might die, and she said the last thing she ever said to me.

Peace Out.

And I've been searching and searching for years, I've been searching, and I love her, and I have to know, I have to know, I have to know. Do you, do you, do you know . . .

Whatever happened . . . to T?

Well, You Look Like a Lesbian

BY SHERRY GLASER

THERE WERE SO MANY BOYS. FROM THE TIME I TURNED thirteen, no twelve. Maybe it was eleven. I was brimming over with sexuality very early in life. I just wanted to play doctor. I liked the touching, the looking, the feelings I got from my body.

I was also deeply insecure. I wasn't pretty or adorable like a lot of my Long Island classmates in the 1970s. I was gangly and had problems with my pale, oily complexion and frizzy hair, and I simply hated my nose. A lot of girls my age were given nose jobs for Bat Mitzvah presents.

My mother said, "Your nose is your nose. It is like no one else's. It makes you you. If you have a nose job it will look like everyone else's, and it will look like you had a nose job. But if you are determined to change your nose when you're eighteen and you have your own money and your own life, you can do that." Since I had to wait patiently to be attractive, I decided to give up the nose job and pursue blowjobs.

This decision was not a healthy one.

kissed again. We couldn't and wouldn't stop kissing. At last, she withdrew and asked me if I wanted to come into her bungalow on the bay.

I got so very shy all of a sudden, like a little girl with her first blush, but I was grown-up, a consenting adult—and the wild combination of that unnerved me.

"Um," I tried to orient myself to the sparkling night, the bay, and get a deep breath. "Yeah, I would, but I'm . . . I have my period. Wow, did I just say that?" I shook my head.

She laughed her goofy high giggle, displaying her overlapping two front teeth, which made her extra adorable.

She said, "I don't mind. I get my period too."

"Right."

She gently grabbed me by my hair and pulled me into her mouth again.

I surrendered.

I'm not going to go into all the super-intimate details of what happened in her luxurious boudoir that night, but I will tell you that there were veils involved. And upon the immeasurable softness of full female immersion, I was profoundly informed by my deepest psyche that THIS is what I like.

I like girls.

Birth Day

BY LEAH LAX

Excerpted from
Uncovered: How I Left Hasidic Life and Finally Came Home

Introduction

WHEN I WAS SIXTEEN, I FELL IN LOVE WITH THE HASIDIM. You've seen them: Jewish ultra-orthodox men in black hats and suits and untrimmed beards, their wives in wigs and modest clothing, more often than not with children in tow. I was a Dallas public-school kid from a sixties liberal home and the world invaded my living room every night on television: Vietnam—guns and body bags, protests, race riots; Catholics and Protestants fighting in Ireland; Israel under siege. And those women burning bras. My family life didn't clarify anything. Where was a peaceful island?

Who was I? Who knows at that age. But I wanted to know. And digging into the old-world religion my immigrant family had left behind for clarity—for a return to an older, simpler truth— seemed a good defiant thing. Besides, I had begun to think that the ache in my chest must be my soul. Maybe, I thought, maybe there is a God.

I had this girlfriend (of course there was a girlfriend) with whom I'd fallen in love, and I didn't dare tell her. We had planned to go camping one weekend but it looked like rain. Instead, we chose the Live and Learn Sabbath Experience at our local synagogue, sponsored by visiting Hasidim who had come offering a taste of their "authentic" Judaism. We went as voyeurs. My life changed because of a caprice in the weather.

Because I fell right in. There is a homoerotic undertow in gender-divided communities, and there was the easy sense of belonging I found there when I had always felt different, since all you had to do was follow the rules and you belonged. And, ever dangling just ahead, was their great, enticing promise of God's eternal love.

Later, at university, I found other Jewish kids equally enamored with the Hasidim (who had conveniently set up an outpost right near campus). But it wasn't just Jewish kids who were turning toward fundamentalism. We were just reflecting a greater sweep to the right and to right-wing religion occurring on campuses across America. I believe this to have been in part, for all of us, our adolescent rebellion.

Soon, I was a new wannabe Hasid moving through the world as if in a glass bubble. You out there became cardboard cutouts, no depth or heart, your voices muted. As an effort to ratify the ERA marched state to state, as new feminists were planning what was going to be a historic convention in Houston, for me, the world receded. The baby lesbian in me became a distant cry.

One day, our rabbi sat me down and proposed a match with a young man in my new community. That I had no such attraction was, of course, irrelevant.

My memoir, *Uncovered*, begins with my wedding, then takes readers deep into my life as a Hasidic wife, mother, and closeted lesbian, because I took my place in the ranks. Over the next ten years, I bore seven children, as birth control was forbidden. My children became my everything.

The following excerpt of *Uncovered* takes place twenty-five years after I left secular society behind, at a time when I had almost forgotten myself. I had just recently met Jane.

BIRTH DAY

AFTER DUSK. We get out of the car and walk quietly into a deserted neighborhood park far enough from my home and sit down on a wooden platform, part of a children's climbing gym. A mosquito whines past. There's a rope bridge, ladders, more platforms, a slide, all mute with child echoes. I wanted more seclusion than this, newly aware of people who may hate us if I decide to hold her, if she cries. Jane slaps at a mosquito on her arm. We get up, cross a path that bisects the park, settle on the other side of a bench in deep shade. She does cry. I put my arm around her delicate shoulder, my palm cupped around her arm. Something in me melts away then in the dusk, old trees folding us into olive-green shadow. As she cries. Resistance, care, leftover propriety for God . . . evaporate.

I pull myself away, but my hand and arm feel painfully empty. I take a deep breath and suggest we walk on. I don't know what I'm doing, or why I lead her. She is in pain, meek, and follows. Trees overhang the dirt path, remaining light filtering through. "I used to bring the kids here when they were small," I say. My ghost children circle on tricycles and dart around us.

At the end of the path is an enormous birdcage standing on the ground, perhaps ten feet by twelve by ten, with swings and perches, dishes of water and seeds, and dozens of exotic birds, so many colors. I'm familiar with them, though the light is so dim here I have to conjure the details. In the shadows the remembered colors are reduced to vague silhouettes and intimations of color.

"Look," I say, at captured beauty, wasted wild luminescence—I want her to be able to see all of it. I project myself among those birds, but imagining being one of them in the cage is unbearable. "I wish I could let them fly," I say. We listen to rustles and coos, the flap of a shadow.

Beyond the birds is a grassy enclave enclosed by walls of tall bushes where my boys once played ball. The moon is out. "We used to call this the secret garden," I say. We settle inside it on another bench in the shadows. Branches above us form black lace across the moon glow. A breeze grows cool. Before I can stop myself, I say, "I'm cold," knowing it's an invitation.

When Jane puts her arm around me, I simply can't take any more, can't just talk and think and hold back like I do every day of my life. Fear slams into me so strong it almost lifts me from the seat, but I know this is it. I may never have this door opened again. I turn and kiss her.

I DON'T SLEEP FOR DAYS. Everything around me is in high resolution, exposed. All my hypocrisies, exposed. The Mexican tile, the kitchen walls covered in washable vinyl I once chose with care, are all disintegrating. Soon I'll be standing in my kitchen in an open wind, alone.

Jane has done nothing, just changed me, so that if I thought I could stay in this sheltered place while remaining newly conscious, I was wrong. Jane had done nothing, just made me admit I'm an alien in my own home, so that now it feels unreal to wake in the morning, prepare a meal, empty the dishwasher, as if I've been violently displaced by someone else. Jane does nothing, just wakes up in the morning at her place and pads alone into her own kitchen for morning coffee, then to the shower, where she lets beads of hot water rain down on supple skin.

The kids speak and I can't hear. Food swirls in my stomach without feeding this hunger. I stop eating after a few bites.

I can't function, can't think.

Which may be why I stand in Jane's house a week later on a Sunday morning, and why she says so little, why we both hardly speak as if we're shy as schoolchildren who have just been introduced. Perhaps it is why I try to keep up the pretense this is just a visit, wanted to say, *Hi, nice place you have. Wanna show me around?* And it is why when we get to the bedroom my brain stops and then we are in the bed and I am holding onto her as if I have to make sure I don't fall. "Teach me," I say, a ridiculous line that makes her laugh, because no one need teach me a thing as all thought melts away. Her softness is a sound that fills my ears. Compared with this, memories of Levi are paper that rustles and scatters. There is no will, no words, just this hum of touch, and her mouth holds paint that outlines my shape on a new canvas. Somehow, the movement of my hand amplifies sound. I have been here for a thousand years, and here I will be. Her body is shaped to fit mine—that's the proof.

Here is where I am born. Oh, my children, how can you ever understand? Your mother was just birthed today.

ANOTHER DAY, ANOTHER MIDNIGHT. I edge open the back door and try to make sure it doesn't creak. I put the car into neutral and slide down the drive with the driver's-side door ajar. Once in the street, I ease the door closed and start the motor so that I could be anyone, a passing car that stalled, a Hasidic mother escaping to her lesbian lover.

Biting my lip, foot on the pedal. There's the crisp night air, nostrils flared, rub of seemingly superfluous clothes on heightened skin, the motor vibrating up my legs and spine and humming through my seat. Cold hard wheel on my palms. I glide through the sleeping Hasidic neighborhood like a reptile, narrowed eyes trained on dark empty streets looking for betrayal, propelled by a body scream. My family shrinks to a pinpoint behind me and blinks out.

There wasn't a narrative anywhere I could find that told that particular story.

I wanted to run and I wanted to hide and I wanted to do anything at all that would make this not be so, anything that would take me back to my safe and predictable life with my future laid out before me.

But a truth like that demands reckoning. And in order to fully know—to quell that burning fire inside me that demanded answers—I had to demolish a life.

I had to smash it and burn it to the ground and stand in the wreckage, and I had no idea how to do it honestly.

So I did it the only way I knew—fast and hard and without much integrity but with a hell of a lot of collateral damage.

It took me years to unpack the guilty weight of our undoing. I carried it all. Because it was all mine.

How do you heal pain that was your own creation?

In the end, it's the words that have always saved me.

There is a belief, in our world, that a chosen grief is not a valid grief.

Grief. It and the small subset of words around it are the dominion of those whose loss was thrust upon them via some external force. I had the gall to try to claim as my own a thing that was reserved for those from whom something had been taken or ripped or stolen.

Because I had chosen to break my life, my family, my home, in search of my own truth, my right to also deeply grieve that end of past and present and future was not mine.

Perhaps I believe this too.

How can you tell your story when you feel like you're stealing words that you don't deserve to use?

What was the ending point? When was it over?

I remember the life we shared, and the love, steadfast and true. I know the kiss I placed on the top of our newly born daughter's head, brand new to this Earth. I know the home we made of each other's body and the exact feel of his hand in mine.

And I know the life I live now, in the aftermath. I know the hard-earned integrity and the truth that is carved deep into my bones. I know the bliss of bodily surrender in a way that I never could have imagined. I know what it is to own my own desire—the heat and salt and sweat of it.

But the section in between is a blur. It stands outside of all the rest, fuzzy-edged and spinning still.

Do I wish I had paid more attention to the end? Yes. I wish I had known—don't we always wish we had warning before devastation? Isn't it human to want to record and replay and remember exactly what was?

If only someone had whispered, *take the time to notice the specifics of your leaving. Pay exquisite attention to the details of what this life has been. One day you will search your mind for the details.*

If only I had known what was to come.

It's strange now, that I remember so little about those final months.

It's funny, isn't it, how seldom we know the last things are the last?

The real grief came later—after the exhilaration and the adrenaline and the meeting of this new self. After the experimentation and the thrill and the unpacking of a life reborn.

The real grief came in the quiet that remained after the wreckage. When everything looked tidy and cleaned and done.

That is when the tears would come late at night and steal me from bed. That is when I would find my wedding album and play the song and sit and cry.

That is when I began to understand that I could have done a thing that was the right thing and the wrong thing, all at once.

When I began to learn that right and wrong are small words that don't even come close to what is.

It seems that you can know, deeply, that this was the inevitable choice. The one that led to truth and wholeness. A road that had to be traveled. And still ache for what was before.

Sometimes there are no choices that do not involve deep loss and deep grief and deep guilt. Some choices are just that—deep. And all you can do is live them through, with as much bravery and truth as you can muster. Even when there isn't much to pull from. Even when the ache beats steadier than your own heart.

Because sometimes what has been gained and what has been lost tangle, sweet and sticky painful, all twirled together and impossible to separate.

Sometimes this is the complicated and painful path to wholeness.

Christmas morning, almost a decade later.

This is not my house. I've spent the night on an air mattress, next to her—the woman I love.

We are in his house—the man I once married in that white country church. The house he shares with this partner.

And we get up and make breakfast in our pajamas. Sharing the duties and navigating the kitchen as if we always do. And we eat the traditional Swedish Tea Ring, made from my mother's recipe, our hands sticky with cinnamon and dried fruit and icing. We record the kids reacting to the mountain of presents that come with two households consolidating on one day.

We give them this. The only thing they really want. All of us all here together. Grace and pain intermingled in ways that can never be untangled.

This, it turns out, is the new life we have built.

And this is not to paint too pretty a picture—to tie this essay with a bow and promise a new sort of happily ever after. But this is to show you the karma of this love. This is to show you that good things can still be made. This is to promise you that you do not have to carry the guilt of what you have done forever.

Where you go, I will go. Where you stay I will stay.

Sometimes even promises broken remain true.

Just One Look

BY DARSHANA MAHTANI

As an Indian daughter in Barbados, I was told who I was before I could figure it out for myself. My whole life was a preamble to marriage. How to budget for groceries, remove greasy stains from marble tables, make chai, entertain and dress accordingly, pay compliments, satisfy my husband, impress the in-laws, and, most importantly, listen without having an opinion—these were the important things to know. It didn't matter to my parents if I was educated or not. But they allowed me to go to community college, to pass the time before I came of age to marry.

There was so much pressure on young Indian girls in the community to be worthy. We had to catch a potential husband's interest with just one look. That's how the men would choose us: with just one look. That's how my father chose my mother and how my grandfather chose my grandmother. Being the eldest granddaughter of both families, I was first in line to marry. I was the example, a role model to my younger brothers and cousins, expected to learn and love that one day a man would swap me for a dowry and depend on me to manage his home and family.

I first heard of this tradition at age six, when my mother caught me stealing a second ice cream sandwich from the freezer.

"Dolly," she said in a gravely serious tone I'd never quite heard before, "I am taking this away for your own good. When you grow up and we must find you a husband, you will thank me for this." She removed the ice-cream sandwich from my sticky hands and threw it in the garbage.

After this incident, she put a lock on the pantry and bought a fridge so tall the freezer was completely out of reach. Something inside me snapped that day. Over the next four years, I became rebellious, resentful of my mother, and mouthed off about not wanting to get married. Having a husband equaled no more ice-cream sandwiches. And I really liked ice-cream sandwiches.

Over the phone, my mother mentioned my uncontrollable rebellion to my grandfather. The next thing I knew, when I was ten years old, they sent me to live with my grandparents in the south of Chile.

The last words my mother said to me when she dropped me off at the airport: "It's for your own good. You will thank me one day, trust me. When you get married, this will all make sense."

My grandfather was a serious man. He had no patience for mistakes, hesitation, doubt, or fear.

Basically, he had no patience for me.

My mother promised I would be staying there only a couple of months, returning home after summer vacation. But it turned out that three months wasn't enough to transform me into a beautiful, elegant swan worthy of a prince. I was still an opinionated duckling, tripping over my own two feet, so I spent five more years living there. I made new friends, learned Spanish, and watched my grandmother die of cancer. I went home when the family felt confident that I had reformed. They instructed me to wait until they found a suitable family for me to marry into. As I waited, I begged them to let me go to school. After one year of begging, they finally said yes, and I proudly became one of the first girls in my community to go to college.

It was there that I met Chloe.

Everyone stopped what they were doing to watch the girl with tattoos walk into class and take her seat. She scouted the room. Then she looked at me.

"Is someone sitting here?" she asked pointing, to the seat next to me.

"No," I blurted out.

She smiled.

"Wow, we've got some sexy ladies this year," I heard a tall, large, dark boy say from the back of the class.

She was definitely sexy. Her skin was the color of burnt caramel. Her hazel eyes pierced me. My heart was in a hurricane; I felt magnetically pulled to her. I needed to be near her, to hold her. The expressions she made, how her laugh filled up the room . . . everything about her drove me crazy.

I caught her noticing my long, black, curly hair.

"You're so lucky. We have to pay real money to get our hair to look like yours," she said, running her fingers through a few loose strands, lighting a flame. The fire started to course through my entire body.

"This is a 100% pure-breed Indian. She's the example of good genes!" she said to the class, looking at me with a smile.

I wasn't sure if that was a compliment. I hesitantly shot her a smile.

"So what's your major?" she asked.

"Management."

"Really? That's a shocker," she said sarcastically with a grin.

"Why?"

"It's what all you Indians study, isn't it?"

It hurt that she looked at me and saw a stereotype.

"Maybe, but I'm not like any other Indian girl you know. What's your major?"

"Marketing."

"Oh." Now I was surprised. She didn't seem the type to go to college and study something safe.

"Yeah, so we have a bunch of classes together except I've got extra marketing stuff."

"Cool."

"I'm Chloe, by the way."

"I'm Dolly."

"What's your real name?"

"What?"

"Your Indian name."

"It's hard to pronounce."

"Try me," she insisted.

"Darshana."

"Darshana," she repeated, trying to see if she could pronounce it correctly.

I loved hearing my name coming from her lips.

By the end of the day, we were partners for a project and she had a permanent seat next to mine in class. We became inseparable. I'd sneak out my bedroom window in the middle of the night to pick her up. We'd go to a twenty-four-hour diner, sit at a bar, order hard drinks, bitch about boys, and ogle football or basketball players. We'd munch on nachos while discussing her latest affair or boy crush. Sometimes we'd weigh in on the news and how fucked up the world had become. We dreamt of creating our own world. We called it our utopia.

Then, it happened. Somewhere between the thrill of designing our new world, the sweet aroma of her perfume, and the burning taste of tequila, I realized that I no longer just liked this girl. I loved this woman. Wholeheartedly. I felt unmoored, with just her hand to keep me from drifting. She had become my everything.

Chloe was my best friend for nine years. In those nine years, I concluded that I was, absolutely, unequivocally and without a shadow of a doubt, gay. I did all the tests online. Google was tired of the million variations of "How do you know if you're a lesbian?" that I typed in. I was stuck. I couldn't confess my feelings to Chloe, and I couldn't tell my parents. Should I accept the unacceptable reality—that I would never be happy?

I had only one option that would save my parents the shame of having a daughter like me, and save me the pain of losing them or living a joyless life. I had to do it before I changed my mind.

One afternoon, I started to climb the wrought-iron gate of our porch, stumbling a few times until I made it onto the roof. I walked to the edge of the roof and looked down at the pavement. I would close my eyes and take one more step. Hesitation kicked in . . .

What if I *lived*?

I sat on the ledge to reevaluate. I couldn't stand a day more of hurting the people I loved. What's the point of a life like this? They will be better off. I was doing the right thing. I stood again.

As I shifted my weight forward, my dad's car drove into the garage downstairs. They saw me. Shameful. If I jumped, they'd rush me to the hospital and I would probably survive—maybe suffer a broken leg. I did not want to survive. I climbed down from the roof, feigned illness, and went to bed.

The next day I didn't have the energy to leave my bed or draw the curtains. I skipped school and ignored all calls. My parents thought I had the flu. No one seemed to notice but Chloe. She left me a dozen messages. She wasn't allowed to visit my house because my mother considered her a bad influence, something to do with her tattoos and black skin, but she came anyway. I didn't answer the door. Everything hurt. I spent an entire week like this before I went back into the world.

My twenty-fifth birthday was in two weeks; I was two years past the ideal marriageable age. My birthday was my mother's opportunity to remind people that I was out there, ready and waiting to be picked. She wanted to throw me a big party, but I didn't feel up to it. Chloe begged me to have dinner with her, even though I told her I didn't want to celebrate. But she had a way of changing my mind. That night, we went to my favorite restaurant. We even dressed up. Chloe wore a flowing floral dress and the necklace I'd given her for Christmas. She looked drop-dead gorgeous. We ordered everything on the menu, including the twelve bottles of different wines they had in stock. She showed me her new tattoo. Roman numerals on her ankle. II · XI · MCMLXXXVII. She'd tattooed my birthday onto her ankle. I started to laugh hysterically. I laughed and screamed until I cried on the floor. (I wish I could take it all back. Remembering it makes me feel so pathetic.) Chloe hugged me. She grabbed the last bottle of unopened wine and two glasses. She picked me up from the floor and literally carried me out to the beach. She poured the wine and started to roll a joint. There must have been some courage sprinkled in with the weed because suddenly, I became unafraid.

"You're amazing," I said to her, looking straight into her eyes and meaning every word of it.

She smiled, looking right back at me and said, "So are you, love."

"Thank you. I love my birthday and my gift. So much better than being at my mother's party."

"Your mother must be pissed."

"I really don't care. All she cares about is herself. Sorry about that embarrassing laugh-cry thing earlier."

"Chill. You sure you're having a good time? Today is all about you," she said with a smile.

"Sweetie, I'm having a great time. The best, actually. There's only one thing that would make today perfect."

"What's that?"

"Kiss me." I said firmly. No hesitation. No fear. No regret.

She chuckled. "Where?" she finally asked.

"You know where. Kiss my heart." I made sure I put my feelings into it.

She looked at me, reading me. In that moment, she knew I was saying words I'd never said before.

"No," she said, looking down at the sand.

"Why not?" I implored.

"Just because."

"Because why?" I pushed.

"Dolly . . . " she said condescendingly.

"I need to hear you say it."

"I can't."

"Please, Clo. Please. Just once. I need to hear you say it," I repeated.

"What do you want to hear?" she asked.

"The truth. That you don't love me the way I love you. You just see me as a friend. That you're not interested," I said in anger.

"I can't." I felt her voice break.

"For Christ's sake, I fucking need you to. Once and for all. I need to unburden myself. It's killing me. I'm dying."

She hid her face in the palm of her hands and started to sob. I'd never seen her like this. Ever.

"Hey . . . I'm sorry. I'm so sorry. Forget I said anything, okay? I was being selfish. Please, just forget it. Please don't cry," I said as I tried to console her.

"I can't say that I don't love you," She blurted out in between the sobbing, "because I do. I love you deeply, D."

She regained composure and proceeded to give a confession that sunk me.

"You don't have a clue. I love you more than anyone in my entire life. I love you more than my fucking mother! You're my everything, D. I'm scared, okay? I know how this ends. I will fuck this up. I will hurt you, and you will hate me. I couldn't bear that.

I can't lose you. You mean too much to me." I could feel the determination in her words. "You're the only one I truly trust. What we have doesn't exist on this planet anymore, it's gone extinct. If we lose this, what hope is there?"

I was paralyzed. Speechless.

"A couple lives together, right? Do you see your mother and father just letting you come live with me?"

I loved the sound of that. A home created by the two of us.

"I don't care what they think. Let's just do it," I said firmly.

"Yeah, right. What about your family? What are you going to tell them? What if they ship you off to India to get married? How am I going to find you?"

I always pictured Chloe crashing my wedding and confessing her love to me just before I took that third trip around the fire and promised myself to some man.

"Babe, we love each other, right? It's not going to be easy but I love you so much. . ."

"What about Troy? He's your boyfriend." Chloe said.

"Troy? Come on. He's a friend."

"He's in love with you."

"Yes, but I'm in love with you. He thinks I could be 'the one,' and he's scared because he knows my parents will choose my husband. He thinks that's set in stone. Plus, I hated kissing him. I just hated it. He tasted like salt. I think I wanted to make you jealous the way Dario makes me."

"Dario? That's so funny," she mused. "We fuck. That's it. He's actually jealous of you— says I put you first."

We both looked at each other and laughed.

"What happens when my pussy wants dick? What if I'm attracted to a man and want to have sex with him?" she asked. My chest tightened.

Maybe I wanted love to win because I'd spent nine years fantasizing about this. Yet, she was right—we would not work out. I didn't know how to love openly, and as long as I lived under my parents' roof and rules I'd be trapped. That was the moment I knew I had to break free. Unchain myself from the shackles of responsibilities passed down through generations of my family.

I had to create a new kind of reality. A life where I was free to love who I wanted. Where I could make decisions based solely on my heart. Where fear wasn't a subtle intruder in every experience. My own utopia.

In that moment, we saw each other with new eyes. The vision of requited lovers. Her eyes were full of sadness and love. She kissed me. It must've lasted less than a minute but in that moment, we were together. In that moment, we lived out a lifetime of love. We were twin flames reunited. We were borderless, timeless, fearless, and present. We were beautiful.

One week later, I came out to my parents. We were having our monthly family meeting in our mother's bedroom. My father discussed the monthly plan for the business, our health, allowance, and savings. My mother made a comment about having to put aside extra money since she had a feeling my wedding day would be coming up soon.

"Your sister is getting married this year. Just watch," my mother declared.

"I don't think she's interested in men," my father added.

"No. That's not true. Right, Dolly? That can't be true. Right?" she looked at me half bewildered and half terrified.

This time I wasn't going to hide.

"It's true, Ma. I have never been attracted to a man. Ever."

"You have a problem. I vote we take you to the doctor, get a few tests and see what can be done," she added without much surprise or outrage. It was clear she'd planned for this long in advance.

"This is not a disease that medication can cure. I'm not sick."

"Um, Dolly, that is not true," my brother said.

"It is true."

"You don't know because you never got checked. There are people who take medicine and are no longer gay, so if you haven't done your research about it then you're very wrong, because people do take hormone medicine and they change back to normal," he continued.

"I'll take you to the doctor and you'll be back to normal," said my mother.

"It's not that simple," I said. "There are gay animals." I was getting mad and desperate.

"Which gay animals are there?" my father asked.

"Look at programs on National Geographic. There are gay penguins and dolphins and birds."

"No!" My family replied in unison.

"In our books, Vishnu is neither male nor female," I yelled.

"Now you're really being dumb," my brother said.

"You've been in the wrong company. I'll take you to the doctor and you will be back to normal," my mother begged.

"There is nothing wrong with me. You are hurting me."

"What do you think you're doing to us?" she asked.

"The problem is, she's been like this her whole life," my brother said.

"Well then, it's your fault," my father said to my mother. "If she had told us when she was ten or eleven years old, maybe we could've fixed it."

"Did you ever see Dolly with a boy?" said my brother.

"She had boyfriends in Chile," my mother said.

"I had no boyfriends in Chile. Where are you coming up with this?"

They looked at me, waiting for a glimmer of hope. This was the moment I was supposed to mention a boy's name. If I had, they would continue to trust that I could be fixed.

I remained silent.

"Okay, fine, what are you going to do?" my father asked with rage in his voice.

"I'm . . . I'm going to live my life, Pa," I said, with pain, yet total conviction, knowing I was standing up for happiness.

"Well, I'm sorry, but you can't do that here. If you are going to insist on living this way then you need to do it elsewhere," he said.

Losing my family was always a possibility. I agreed to make a plan, but they still insisted I had to leave home immediately. I felt disowned. I took my pain and shame and turned it into purpose. I decided to move to a more gay-friendly country, and chose Argentina. I hoped I would reunite with Chloe there—eventually.

And that's what I did. I left and made myself into someone who could settle down with a girl I loved someday. I made myself into someone who could be happy and gay, out and proud, authentic. It wasn't easy. My freedom and happiness came at the price of losing my family (temporarily), but it was worth it. I was willing to take the risk of being hurt or rejected or unloved or defeated. Whatever comes my way, I'll face it. My happiness is worth the risk.

No

BY AMANDA MEAD

"NO, YOU'RE NOT."

That was how my mother responded when, at age twelve, I told her I was gay.

Of all the responses in the world, that was not the one I expected. As I sat slack-jawed at the kitchen counter, she continued stirring a simmering pot. Then she turned to me and asked a follow-up question.

"Why in the world would you even *think* you're gay?" she said as she rolled her eyes.

A million thoughts ran through my head, most of which involved pornographic images of girls' bodies. I certainly couldn't tell my mother about *that*, I thought, so I said the next best thing.

"I like to look at other girls?" I said, uncertainly.

"Oh, Amanda," my mother said in true exasperation. "Every girl looks at every other girl. That doesn't mean you're *gay*."

With that one statement, my mother created a not-gay monster. If looking at girls didn't make me gay, then kissing girls also didn't make me gay. I was sure that every girl kissed every other girl. It was just something we do. Neat! I made sure to let my kissing partners know that we weren't gay. When the kissing morphed into fondling, I knew that wasn't gay either. We were just experimenting—learning, even—so that we would be better for the boys once they came knocking on our doors. Some nights, I slipped my fingers past the delicate band of my friends' underwear. That was also not gay. Nope. Not gay at all. Or the friend who had an obsession with being "almost caught," and so would make me lick her on the loveseat in my parents' living room as my mother cooked dinner in the adjacent kitchen? Perfectly hetero.

I didn't just live in denial. I lived in an entirely different universe, one in which I had been given implicit permission to be as gay as I could possibly be and yet not be gay. I had boyfriends, therefore I was not gay. And while I was in those relationships, I didn't fuck girls, so I was easily able to pat myself on the back for my not-gayness. It wasn't until I was in college that I started to waver in my steadfast belief that I was definitely not gay.

I had a great boyfriend. He was sweet, cute, kind, ambitious, and an excellent student. My mother adored him. He knew I liked to look at girls. In fact, for our very first Valentine's Day, he gave me an Angelina Jolie calendar. I started to claim the title "bi-curious." However, I still wasn't gay. Being gay meant you had to be in a relationship with a girl. There was *no way* I could ever *date* a girl. Girls were so dramatic, and obviously I was above that. All of my friends were boys! Girls were just too much.

As obnoxious as this made me, it worked, at least for a while. I was able to placate both my desire for women and my desire to be good. I fantasized about women when I had sex, but that didn't make me gay. Eventually, I married the boy who gave me the calendar, even though every cell in my body was screaming at me that something wasn't right.

We had stopped having regular sex even before the wedding. Our wedding night filled me with dread. I knew I would have to have sex with him. I bought lingerie, we rented the best hotel room my tiny Montana hometown had to offer, and we had perfunctory sex. As soon as it was over, I breathed a sigh of relief.

Over the course of the seven years we were together, our sex life dwindled to nothing. I started to wonder if I was, in fact, actually gay. I was so fundamentally unhappy that my husband agreed to have an open marriage with me. I think in his mind two girls having sex wasn't "real" sex and therefore I wasn't "really" cheating on him.

Then I met a girl, a messy college freshman who was still a teenager. I was in my final year of college (my sixth, in fact) and had no business being an adolescent again, but there I was, reliving what it was like to fall in love for the first time.

I was at an impasse. No longer could I deny that at least part of me was definitely gay. I was sure that not every girl fell in love with other girls. Deep down I wondered if I wasn't *all* gay.

So I did what I always did. I turned to my best friend for advice, who happened to be my husband.

One afternoon we tried to have sex. He couldn't maintain an erection, and I was crying. We were a fucking mess. He laid back on the pillow and put my head on his chest. He quietly sobbed and explained that he was under a lot of pressure at work and school. He asked me why I cried during sex. I turned my head up to him and I said maybe I was *just* gay. I meant that I thought I was all-the-way gay, no-turning-back gay, this-is-over gay. But I used the word maybe and my voice lifted at the end of the sentence, as if I was asking him to confirm or deny it.

"I don't think you're gay," he said. "You just aren't."

My mother said I wasn't gay. My husband said I wasn't gay. Soon enough, my therapist told me I wasn't gay—she insisted that I had a twisted view of my own sexuality because I was a victim of childhood sexual abuse. Friends insisted I wasn't gay as well. I had worked so hard at proving I wasn't gay that everyone believed it. Everyone but me.

When I finally worked up the courage to come out once and for all, I had distanced myself from everyone I loved. I prepared for the blows, and the blows came. I lost those friends who insisted I wasn't gay. I lost my mother, whose dismissal of me was swift and brutal. She felt as though my coming out was a personal attack on her. She largely stopped speaking to me, but when she did, it was through clenched teeth.

My husband tried to continue to stifle his own pain in order to be the gracious man he always was, and to help me be secure and happy in my new identity. Eventually, though, having a relationship of any kind with me wasn't healthy for him, and I lost him, too.

Those losses, though, were eclipsed by the relief of finally being free from the prison of uncertainty about my sexuality. I felt stronger and more confident every day. I stopped listening when people said, "No, you're not." No was not an option. No could fuck off.

I met a woman in the summer of 2008 while I was in Pittsburgh for a job orientation. Abbie was charismatic, intimidating, masculine, and sexual—and she had the best smile I had ever seen. We had intense and immediate chemistry. The night we met, she was out with her best friend, a man she had known since they were both in diapers. In the loud, crowded karaoke bar that would later become her uncle's restaurant, she leaned over to me and told me her best friend was going to be her sperm donor when she was ready to be a mother. In an email early in our relationship, she told me that her coming out didn't change a thing—she still wanted the picket fence, the kids, the house, the classic American dream, just with a woman. She knew exactly who she was and what she wanted.

One visit to Pittsburgh, during dinner with her mother and stepfather, Abbie off-handedly mentioned something about her vision for her future family, when her mother stopped eating and looked at her.

"You're gay," she said. "You don't get to have a family."

When she got over the immediate shock, Abbie explained that there were many ways she could have children—though she knew that wasn't what her mother meant. They argued over the subject, with her mother repeatedly letting her know that her choice to be gay meant she was choosing not to be a mother. Her mother was rejecting her, just as mine had.

From that moment on, I was determined to prove her mother and my mother and everyone who felt the same way wrong. I had listened to "no" too many times before and wasn't keen on backing into another closet. As soon as we were financially stable enough, I was going to make Abbie a mother. I had never had a desire to be pregnant or have a baby, but she did. Even before we married, I started researching fertility clinics and sperm donors and home pregnancy methods for lesbians and the costs of artificial insemination and in-vitro fertilization (in case we ever wanted to extract and fertilize one of my eggs that she would then carry). We looked into foster care, foster-to-adopt, and private adoption. But we didn't move forward. Not with any of the options. We had started a business that was struggling, and we were mired in debt.

In the spring of 2015, we made the decision to become foster parents. I had been working as a public-school teacher for eight years and had been really affected by the students with difficult home lives. I wanted to do more than just listen to kids' stories at school. I wanted to be able to help a child, or many children, in a tangible and significant way. And becoming foster parents, we felt, would honor this personal obligation while allowing us to "try on" parenting.

When Abbie first told her mother about our decision, she was vehemently opposed to it. Over the years since that initial conversation at the dinner table, Abbie and her mother had made significant progress towards repairing their relationship and finding ways to connect, but her reaction to our decision to foster was hurtful and disappointing. She later recognized and apologized for her negative response, but in the meantime, it fueled us to be the best damn foster parents the world had ever seen, just like in the show *The Fosters*. We were going to be the real life Steph and Lena.

Our first child was placed with us that fall. He was a former student of mine who had been abandoned by his birth family. At age thirteen, he was extraordinarily polite and well-mannered. He held open doors and said, "Yes, ma'am." We swelled with love for him.

The honeymoon period was short-lived, however. Our parenting styles clashed, and I believe that our foster child took advantage of opportunities to pit us against each other. My years as a teacher helped me recognize when and how he was manipulating both of us, and I tried, desperately, to help Abbie see it too. Even though she understood what he was doing, she couldn't bring herself to be mad at him or call him out. She said he'd been hurt enough. I told her that we weren't hurting him by teaching him right from wrong. She understood this in theory, but she couldn't bring herself to hold the line. Our relationship was crumbling under the weight of how bad we were at parenting together.

I started to ask myself if I actually wanted to be a parent, or if my desire was borne out of my quest to prove our mothers wrong. On an even bigger scale, I wondered if I was trying to show the world that we were just like straight people; we were just as *good*. If that were true, if it were true that my motivations for becoming a parent were inherently selfish, then maybe I shouldn't be one, I rationalized. And if I truly didn't want to be a parent, then maybe

Abbie and I weren't meant to be together, because I knew from the very minute we met that's who she was and what she wanted.

Finally, one night, I let it all go. I told her how I felt about everything. To my surprise, she told me she wasn't sure she wanted to be a parent either. She liked us as just the two of us. Plus, our business was starting to do well, and she wanted to devote herself to it. The idea of pregnancy was no longer something she really wanted. We were just starting to climb out of our mountain of debt, and we could see vacations in our future. We could maybe buy a house, visit her family once a year, and go to some of the places we'd always wanted to see together. That is, if we didn't have children. We held hands, we cried a bit, and we were thankful our foster son was visiting his father overnight.

Our foster son moved in with his father permanently in June 2016. The process of reuniting with his father was painful for everyone involved, but especially for our foster son. He had never lived with his biological father, as prior issues with addiction and illness had rendered his father unable to care for him. But after seven years of sobriety and stability, he was pursuing custody. The judge in his case unexpectedly asked one of us to share with the court whether or not we supported reunification with his father. Foster parents, by design, do not have a voice in the court system, but there we were, forced to stand up in court, face our son, and tell him we believed he should leave our home for his father's. He felt deeply betrayed.

"Well, I guess you got what you wanted," he said to me on the car ride home. I bit my lip, gripped the steering wheel a bit tighter, and tried not to notice his stifled sobs. There was a certain amount of truth in what he said. We were ready for him to leave.

Abbie and I are still actively involved in his life, and in some ways we've grown closer to him since he left. This, I am convinced, would not have been possible if he still lived with us. I'm not sure there would *be* an us if he still lived in our home.

We considered all of the scenarios of parenthood again. Maybe if we changed our age range to younger kids, we would have better luck. Maybe if we raised a child from infancy it would be easier. Or maybe if the child were biologically ours. . . . We haven't completely answered these questions; we decided we wouldn't make a final decision just yet. But we've stayed up late many weekend nights discussing how much we enjoy each other's company, without interference. It's a selfish point of view, of course. But that's okay with me now. It took us a while, but we realized that our hesitancy to move forward with parenthood sooner was a sign that perhaps, deep down, we never really wanted that for us. We are still trying to sort out the complicated mess of what really are our individual desires and which ones we created out of rebellion or the need to feel good enough. Queers are used to being told no. No, you don't belong here. No, you can't have that. No, you aren't worthy. This time I'm the one saying no. No, I don't think this is right for me.

Maybe. I'm not sure.

I am still learning when to hear and believe the word no, even if I'm the one saying it.

Straightening Myself Out

BY PAT CROW

I HAD BEEN MARRIED FOR THIRTY-ONE YEARS WHEN I WAS jarred out of a sound sleep by a dream about my friend and houseguest, Ana, standing naked next to my bed. When I opened my eyes, I suddenly longed to climb the spiral staircase, enter the loft where she slept, and caress her ample bosom.

I lay awake the rest of the night in shock, afraid of what this meant. I wondered, am I really attracted to her? Does this make me a lesbian? Am I . . . *gay?*

The following morning my husband, Arthur, left for his commute to work in Orlando. As Ana and I chatted, I couldn't stop, like a teenage boy, looking at her breasts. She noticed my noticing and looked at me, bewildered. I was even more bewildered.

My mind raced beyond Ana's breasts to the larger questions of how I was going to get out of a stagnant, abusive marriage and how it would affect my children, who, though adults of twenty-five and twenty-six, would certainly have questions of their own.

I'm a fourth-generation Floridian with lineage dating back to the Civil War era. Though I couldn't say homophobia was in my blood, I had certainly been acculturated with it through my white-bread, straight, provincial youth—with little to no exposure to gay people—and my Southern Baptist upbringing. "It's not God's way," was the mantra, and the accompanying vision of perpetually burning in hell was enough to stifle my instincts as I unconsciously slid into my role as a traditional southern lady.

Looking back, I remember leaving my body when I had to be in distasteful situations in the bedroom so that I didn't have to feel my discomfort. Drinking lots of wine was one way I left. Getting lost in projects where I disconnected from everything around me was another way I disassociated.

About twenty years into my marriage, I started budding as a feminist and felt resentful of the moral mandate to subjugate myself to my man and my marriage. I read a passage in the prologue of *The Mists of Avalon,* by Marion Zimmer Bradley, that riveted me: "I have no quarrel with the Christ, only with his priests who called The Great Goddess a demon and denied that she ever held power in this world." I read other feminist books as well and became restored as a sovereign woman with dominion over my thoughts. My blood boiled in rage at the misbegotten power of the men in my life.

As a husband and as a father, Arthur demanded the same reverence he learned to show for his Methodist parents. When I didn't fall in line, he told me I was overreacting, getting too big for my britches, or that I didn't know what I was talking about. The last straw: when he held his hand in front of my face, saying, "You don't get to talk. There's something wrong with you," at a restaurant with our adult children.

Soon after my dream about Ana, I visited my sister and told her that I broke the news to Arthur about wanting a divorce because I had changed so much that I could no longer be true to myself and stay in the marriage.

For hours we chewed on how my marriage had disintegrated. "You better start packing and get the heck out of there because right now he's in shock," she said. "When he comes around he's going to be madder than a trapped alligator, and it could get ugly!"

Soon after the Obama family moved into the White House, my divorce became final, and I moved to Port Townsend, Washington, the farthest point from Orlando that I could find on the map.

In a stroke of luck, the neighborhood where I rented a home on the Olympic Peninsula turned out to be a vibrant lesbian community. Most of the women there had already coupled up, making it both easier and more challenging for me because I was of two minds. I was curious about dating women but didn't think I was grounded enough to try. I was shy about my newfound sexuality—not at all ready for a fling, let alone a relationship.

My adjustment wasn't easy. As a straight married woman, I had been part of a club that allowed me to enter places without question. Now I was unattached, new to a very different neighborhood, and not included in social gatherings. I watched from my window as groups of paired-off lesbian friends gathered in their backyards to party on the Fourth of July and Labor Day. For the first time, I longed to belong the way I did with my family back in Florida.

I hungrily watched every nuance of interaction with these women: their affections, their arguments, their bodies, their activities, even how they dressed and carried themselves. What stood out for me was how supportive of one another they were. They had each other's backs in work, play, and everyday living. There was nothing extraordinary that separated me from them. This subculture of lesbians had thrived parallel to me most of my life, yet I didn't acknowledge it until I identified with it because of my encapsulated upbringing. Once my cage door opened, my Christian mores disappeared, and I could see beyond the confines of my redneck, judgmental rearing.

I was fifty-nine years old and, ironically, the baby dyke on the block. They had a history I didn't share. I hesitated to jump into the group, pulling back when someone moved too fast in my direction.

I felt safe coming out to Jane, one of the community's social leaders, first, since she seemed understanding and warm. She made sure to include me in their gatherings, and I began to teach local classes in energy psychology and somatic psychotherapy.

Zoe, an old lesbian colleague and friend from the Northeast, stayed in touch with me during my adventures. She was in the process of ending a long-term relationship and was planning to move to Santa Fe, New Mexico. She supported my transitions along the way, asking every detail of my encounters. She had been out for over thirty years and was curious about my experiences amongst my northwestern neighbors. I confided in her how insecure I felt. She laughed with joy when I told her that finally I was ready to date—as if she had been waiting to hear this from me—and a tacit doorway opened.

Let it go, I thought to myself. *You're too far away to even think of starting anything with her.* We continued to chat daily, and our friendship became more intimate. Months later, she mailed me a Barbra Streisand CD. When I was on the phone talking with her about the songs I liked, I realized she was reaching into my heart through them. My throat clenched, and I heard myself say to her, "I think I'm falling in love with you." Silenced by my own words, I heard her soft voice respond, "You have no idea how much I love you, Pat." My illusion of not feeling ready to act on being gay evaporated. I was in love with another woman.

After several months of phone sex, we planned a rendezvous in Santa Fe where we would consummate our new love. She brought me out with abandon, and I just let go. The rest of the week, we toured the rural roads of northern New Mexico, sharing romantic nights in funky Madrid and Taos and discovering Ojo Caliente's private pools. The moon was full that week, and in the middle of the night Zoe woke me from a deep sleep to make love. I hadn't felt so alive in well over a decade. My libido was on fire and I think it scared her. At dinner in Taos one evening she ordered a head of roasted garlic. "I'm eating this whole garlic. Watch. Maybe this will slow you down some."

"No garlic will stop me!" I teased.

There was an elegant difference about making love with a woman as opposed to a man. Her skin was soft and supple. I got aroused from kissing her lips and fondling her breasts. A man's skin was rough. His physique was hard. I got aroused from his efforts, not from my own pleasure of touching. I couldn't stop stroking Zoe and feeling my whole body breathe heavily. Her tenderness moved me. We fit together perfectly.

Then she came to Port Townsend to spend a week with me. Again, we tumbled into bed with unbridled passion. One day, I took her for a low-tide tour of the cape and found a private rock to climb on to make out until the tide rose. The next day I took her to land's end at Cape Flattery where we lost touch with the world.

When it was time for her to return home, I didn't want to break the spell of our glorious memories, so the two-hour trip into Seattle to the airport was quiet. On the ferry ride, surrounded by the windy surf, the breeze caught her silver hair. It glistened in the sun. I took in her soft butch essence, appreciating how handsome she was. When I walked back into my empty house, I felt a void, loud and quiet at the same time. Everything vibrated with her energy. My bereft heart pondered. *How do I make a new life for myself here when I want to share it with her?*

I felt overwhelmed with loneliness and decided to call my daughter, Rikki, in Oregon and come out to her about Zoe. She was supportive and curious.

During my first Christmas alone in Port Townsend, phone conversations and e-mails with Zoe kept me going, but I was lost. Trying to build a new life in a new place with my lover so far away was like trying to build a house without nails. In every contact I made and every class I taught, my body was there but my spirit was in New Mexico. Something had to give.

In the aftermath of Japan's tsunami and Fukushima's nuclear power plant meltdown in March 2011, Zoe insisted I come to Santa Fe. The threat and fear of radiation poisoning worried us both. We set a plan in motion. She offered to come to Port Townsend and drive with me.

In Santa Fe, Zoe lived at Rainbow Vision, an LGBT retirement residential center. We decided to be together in separate apartments while we got to know each other better and tried on our new relationship. A year and a half went by, and I went back to Florida to see family and friends. I came out to my ex-husband and son. My ex said he wasn't entirely surprised, but he felt humiliated. My son was open-minded, but worried about how others would take it.

On June 26, 2013, the Supreme Court struck down the Defense of Marriage Act, opening the door for LGBT movement toward legal and sustainable marriage. On June 26, 2015, the Supreme Court declared marriage equality the law of the land, creating a frenzy of same-sex marriages. Wedding fever ensued in Santa Fe and all over the country. I welled up with joy for this entire population of people who had wanted to be treated equally all their lives. One lesbian friend said to me, "I feel like a whole human being now." A sense of pride came over me when I realized that I was part of a historical and progressive cultural acceptance of being gay in America.

Almost a year to the day after the Marriage Equality Act was made law, a group of LGBTQ Latino folks were dancing and celebrating in the Pulse night club of Orlando when a maniac plowed forty-nine of them down point blank with an assault rifle like they were tin cans on a fence. I was in Oregon with family, celebrating my daughter's graduation from college. The next morning, as we were slowly waking up from the party and drinking our coffee, we saw flashing blue-and-red lights on the TV with the headlines on the screen, "49 Dead in Orlando Massacre." My mind didn't register what had happened until Rikki began checking in with her Orlando friends on Facebook to see if they were safe. One by one she called out their names, reporting their status. My daughter-in-law, Noel, and my son, Gareth, let us know they were okay. But Noel said she was worried about her cousin, Dani, and his husband, Jean, because she knew they were at the club that night.

I felt my focus shift from the excitement of Rikki's celebration to the gravity of the unfolding tragedy. Her untouched graduation cake sat on the table along with several unopened cards. And by day's end, we had confirmation that Dani and Jean were killed in the shooting. My heart sank, knowing that this horrible, devastating event would forever change the lives of everyone connected to the dead.

This tragedy made me all the more eager to get back to my love in Santa Fe. Zoe picked me up from the airport in Albuquerque, and later that evening we went to the plaza downtown to partake in a vigil for the Pulse victims. Our openly gay mayor, Javier Gonzales, city council members, and gun control advocates all spoke in honor of the dead. As we stood there, my numbness kept me from acknowledging my own pain. A lesbian friend approached us and said she kept looking around to see if it was safe for her to be out in the open amongst her gay friends. It finally struck me why gay folks were always warily looking over their shoulders. Even with the recent successful Supreme Court battles, there was nothing sanctified about being gay. In fact, I realized, being gay was still very dangerous.

For the first time, I felt what other gay people lived—a fear of being out. Once I stepped out of my armor, believing finally that it was safe to do so, homophobic hatred punched me in the gut. I had been out for only five years, and at sixty-five I felt apprehensive about my safety. And with our new president-elect, Donald Trump, choosing his cabinet, I question whether the strides made for the LGBT community will remain intact. I can see that more battles lie ahead.

But I recognize my courage to break free from my stifled life in Florida, and recent legal victories have enabled me to live a life congruent with my sexual identity. A freer life. A *happier* life. Recently, Zoe and I got married in our backyard, celebrating with a handful of good friends and our two rescue dogs, dressed in fancy pink and rainbow-colored collars. Santa Fe is a bubble of liberal-minded LGBT residents. It's called "The City Different" for good reason.

Pregnant with Myself

CASSIE PREMO STEELE

ALL MY LIFE, I'VE WANTED TO BE GOOD.

My last boyfriend before my husband was a kind Irish Catholic man from Connecticut. He was a virgin. I was not.

He had the soft hands of a priest. He was so sweet he ate sugar sprinkled on his spaghetti. I would drink a beer before he came to pick me up for a date because he was so nice. And nice, to me, was boring.

But I could see us marrying. I could see us living in New England, having children, sending them to the nearby Catholic school, settling down for quiet nights at home like his parents. It seemed so normal. So calm. Like a balm over my promiscuous, wounded heart. It would be a way for me to be good, too.

We didn't marry, though. Instead, I became pregnant by someone else.

We had only had sex once, under the covers in February, furtively grasping in the dark while my grad-school roommate slept in the room next door.

Six weeks later, having declined an offer to enter the Peace Corps after a phone interview conducted from bed while eating saltines and trying not to throw up, I began to have sharp pains in my belly.

I had gone to my mom and stepdad's house that weekend. I was twenty-four, but I needed them to know that I was pregnant. They offered to let me live with them. They offered to help with the baby. My stepfather, a wonderful cook and the true wife of the house, made me my favorite French onion soup with extra gooey cheese, and then I went to bed.

At first I thought it was indigestion. But the pain was so intense I screamed and blacked out repeatedly before consciously registering that it was pain.

The next day I went to the university's student health center and they sent me—alone, in my roommate's borrowed car—to the ER, where they admitted me immediately and started prepping me for a laparoscopy to remove what turned out to be an ectopic pregnancy.

Before I knew it, my mom was there. And my priest, a kindly British man who would later be kicked out of the priesthood for being too forgiving. He knew me from the Catholic Student Center where I taught an independent course on homelessness.

"What happened?" he said with a smile.

I had no words. I pointed at my belly. He nodded.

I so wanted to be good.

All my life, I've wanted to be a mother. My birth name is Mary, and for a young girl in a small Minnesota town with Catholic parents, being a mother and being good seemed like very good things to want.

At the age of eight, I was raped by a neighbor.

I checked my pee daily for weeks afterward, wondering if I could tell from the color if I was pregnant. I stole mothering magazines from my pediatrician's office to learn how to do it well just in case.

To be good.

After the ectopic pregnancy, the laparoscopy scar was a six-inch straight line across my belly just above my pubic hair. It hurt for months. Not the scar exactly, but the inside parts, cutting sharp crosses from time to time within me.

In only six weeks, I'd gone from not being pregnant to being pregnant to not being pregnant again. I envisioned the pregnancy leaving tire marks on the ovary and remaining fallopian tube and uterus as it left my body so quickly. I imagined the pain was a way of washing the marks. Cleansing me. So I could be good.

When I was in high school, it was exciting for me to know I might get pregnant. As a Catholic girl, even without penetration, I found the proximity of my boyfriend's wet pleasure to my own opening stimulating. Dangerous. Sexy.

I hated being on birth control pills. They made me feel puffy and slow and disconnected from my body. When I broke up with my college boyfriend and stopped using them, I felt juicy and alive again. I remember thinking, "This must be how lesbians feel."

And once I was married, but before my husband and I were trying to get pregnant, there was nothing that turned me on more than to delay the opening of the condom wrapper, enticing him to stay in me, pulling me to higher and higher plateaus, and mountains, and delectable valleys below.

The pinnacle was reached when I conceived. Unlike others who start to grow weary of copulating for a baby, I reveled in it. I did not heed the advice to wait twelve—some said twenty-four—hours between attempts to "let the sperm build up." I wanted it, again and again, over and over.

I see now how my connection between desire and fertility was born of shame. All the years of nuns saying that sex was meant for married people to make babies and anything else was sin—all of this sunk in and froze me underneath my skin.

The only time I felt truly sexy, without guilt or fear, was when I was trying to get pregnant. And once I was pregnant, large and oval and out in the open, I felt an incredible kind of power as men looked at me on the street and I knew they knew I had had sex—and that I'd done it without shame—because here was the proof, in my body, that it was the right kind of sex, that I was a good girl.

When I became pregnant with my daughter, it was discovered that I have a heart-shaped uterus. The baby's body develops in the womb of the mother through folding and unfolding until becoming whole—this is why we are mostly symmetrical, with two arms, two legs, two nostrils, two ears.

In most cases, the uterus starts out in the fetus as a heart-shaped organ and widens into an oval. Mine didn't. So my daughter, from 20 weeks of gestation, had her head stuck in the upper right curve of my heart-shaped uterus.

What this meant, according to the laws of my state, was that I couldn't have a natural birth with a midwife but had to schedule a C-section. I tried everything I could to turn the baby—acupuncture, moxibustion, massage, visualization, hand stands in a pool, legs up the wall —but I decided not to have a doctor try to move her manually. This could have resulted in a sudden onset of labor or damage to the baby or me.

The surgeon used the laparoscopy scar to open me and take out the baby—a wide-mouthed, vernix-laden, beautiful daughter.

So now the scar was a little wider. A little deeper. And once again, it hurt.

The baby was ten months old and I was taking aerobics classes when I approached the instructor shyly.

The scar's placement had cut the muscles of my abdomen so

I had a little C-section pouch that hung over my pubic area, and despite months of sit-ups and crunches, it wouldn't go away.

The aerobics instructor was a perky southern blonde who weighed about ninety-five pounds. But I knew she had children. So I asked her advice on tightening the belly.

"Oh, honey," she said. "Do what I did. Get a tummy tuck."

I walked away and went to pick up my daughter from the child-care room, blinking back tears, remembering the words of the surgeon during my post C-section appointment when I tried to complain about the way the belly flopped down.

"Your baby has a cute, floppy belly," he said. "Now you do, too."

I was pissed. I felt like the patriarchy had come in and knifed me in the belly and here I was, trying to get rid of the belly, but resentful that the solution I was being offered was another knife and another surgeon.

I went home and ate a pint of ice cream on the kitchen floor with my daughter.

Over the course of my sixteen-year marriage, I gained eighty pounds. When I look back at early pictures of us together now, it's not my youth that strikes me. It's how thin I am.

Part of the reason I gained the weight was because I became a wife. I cooked dinner and bought the groceries—on a budget of $400 a month, which he deposited for me in a joint checking account. I shopped first at home the way a financial counselor taught me to do, looking in the fridge and cabinets for what was already there, using that to create a meal plan for the week; then I made a list; then I shopped at the cheapest places, splurging only occasionally, like when we were having a dinner party.

I was a good wife.

But I would admittedly squirrel away food only for me. Chips. Chocolate. Beer. Pizza for late-night binges after everyone was asleep. I did most of my eating in bed while my husband worked in his study. I was in the dark. Alone.

The true end of my marriage began months before I fell in love with a woman. It was Thanksgiving of the year before that I decided to go on the Virgin Diet. I eliminated wheat, dairy, soy, corn, peanuts, sugar, and artificial sweetener—which was meant to halt the inflammation caused by food intolerances, reset my taste buds, and rewire the way my body responded to food. I began to feel lighter. I grew tolerant of the feeling of hunger. I began to feel the life in the fruits and vegetables I ate. My body began to feel awake.

My body began to feel good.

Twenty-three years later, that Irish Catholic man is still my friend.

In a Facebook message to him after I came out, I wrote: "Always before, with men, I felt that the desire was a bridge to what I truly wanted, which was love. Now I know that when the love comes first and bursts forth in overwhelming acceptance and kindness, the desire springs from that. That's the difference. That's how I know I am gay and this is me and truly right for my life."

Just as you cannot fully savor the crunch of a salad when your mouth is still reeling from the salt and fullness of a bag of vinegar potato chips, I did not know what desire was when I was with men. Yet as I kissed Susanne, as I moved my hands over the soft plane of her hips, as I felt her enter me, wetter than I had ever been, I realized that the moves I made with men in bed were always a kind of performance.

Move this limb. Feel that. Close your eyes and let yourself be washed away. Focus. Go far away, into a fantasy. Always this motion between mind and body—always this separation between the doing and the desiring—leading up to a point. The point of his entering. The point of his coming. The impossible point of orgasm without some help from my own hand.

Performance and transaction. For the journey was not as important as the destination and end result. The ring. The calmness he felt afterwards. The closeness. The baby. The dinner out so I didn't have to cook. The help folding the laundry.

The other day, while driving home from getting groceries, I heard Mary Chapin Carpenter's song, "He Thinks He'll Keep Her," and burst into tears. Although I had owned the CD and listened to it during my marriage, I had not really understood the song. Until I left, I never saw how hard I was trying to be good.

The homemade meals. The laundry. The seasonal porch decorations. The Christmas cards. The mopping. The gardening. The school pickup. The flowers at the center of the table.

Sitting in the driveway of the house I now own with my wife, I thought back to those years of being good, and I mourned my own failure. It felt like being a captive and then realizing you had the key all along.

Because the truth is I really did want to be a good wife and mother. I really did enjoy making the house into a loving home. I really did take pride in meals cooked mindfully and laundry folded carefully. I still do—even now, married to a woman.

So what is the difference between my former desire to be good, which eventually felt stifling and injurious to my spirit, and my enjoyment of my current life, which, from the outside, has me doing many of the very same actions each day?

In poet Mary Oliver's most recent book of essays, *Upstream*, she writes about what she calls "the third self." There is the child self (the inner, emotional part of ourselves), and the social self (the one concerned with time and food and social arrangements), and then there's a third self for the artist. She encourages readers to ignore the first two selves so that the creative work can get done.

The problem is that this isn't an option for mothers.

Especially mothers who want to be good.

As mothers, we raise all three selves in our children, and this means we can put our own creative desires on a back burner. Or burn them up so completely that the fire alarm goes off. When we are not getting the emotional support we need, we will forego nurturing our third selves in order to keep the first and second selves fed as we tend to our children.

And the anti-mothering rhetoric of certain feminisms is not a solution either, for most women would say that mothering brings them the greatest joy of their life—exactly because it is work—the work of serving and nurturing.

I am still a wife and still a mother. But my new marriage is one of serving and nurturing and supporting the third self in both of us, equally. Marriage that has an unequal level of nurturing for that third self will end up as performance and transaction. It is the third self of our creative, philosophical, and spiritual beings, woven into the social and economic necessities of existence, that will sustain both individuals and the marriage itself.

When I was pregnant, everyone knew I had had sex. Yet I was untouchable. What was the point? I was already pregnant. No man could give me what I already possessed within myself.

I loved it. The combination of visible sexuality and protection. The power of being a creating body yet beyond the objectifying gaze.

The first time I left the house in my newly unpregnant body without the baby, I felt cold and empty, once again at the mercy of the gaze of men who either admired or ignored me. I was an object again to be conquered or critiqued.

And then when I came out, I became pregnant with myself. Those men who knew I was a lesbian looked at me, and I did not look away. Yes, I have had sex. Yes, I have made choices that allow me to have sex that I enjoy. And no, I do not need you for that.

I was no longer an object. I became a creating and desiring body as I had been when I was pregnant. But this time, it was myself I was holding within me. Myself I was birthing. Myself I finally saw as good. Myself I was eating to feed and grow and nurture and please.

I had never felt so free.

Many heterosexual women still live under performative and transactional conditions of desire—in their bodies, in their hungers—where food and sex are connected to money. The truth is that at some level, that obstetrician was right when he told me I would have to learn to love my cute, floppy belly. Because while we can and should respond to heterosexual objectification, rape culture, and gendered structures of economic inequality with rage and blame, this is, I have come to see, only a necessary part of the process toward waking to our own true desire and power. The next steps lead us to loving ourselves and our bellies, our scars, our wounds, and our histories.

I know now what it feels like to make love without wanting something in return. And I know now what it means to prepare and eat a meal without feeling like I am working to earn my keep.

Until I made love with Susanne, I had no idea what desire was. It was like I did not know how to eat until I let myself feel hunger. I am not sure if I would have discovered this about my own desire if I had stayed with men.

When Susanne's body is next to mine and the only exchange between us is something equal—from our mouths, from our lips— it is as if I am finally having a conversation after being a student in a class for all my life.

I no longer have to raise my hand. I no longer must complete the assignment. I will no longer be graded. I no longer have to listen to lectures—long and boring and dull.

Because with each word that I utter and each sentence that I write, I feel myself growing lighter. I no longer fear famine. I am comfortable with hunger. I no longer live under scarcity. I am full, and I have more than enough. There is more than enough in myself and in the community I am helping to create. In my mind and body, belly and heart, I am finally good.

In Defense of Family

BY CARLA SAMETH

AFTER I SPLIT UP WITH MY BABY'S DAD WHEN MY SON WAS eight months old, I decided I really preferred women. I used to think that attraction was more about the individual than about his or her gender. But while I hadn't put myself in the path of many lesbians, I'd felt this attraction since I was eleven years old. I had my first girl experience with my best friend in high school after sharing a bottle of Southern Comfort.

When my son, Raphael, was about five years old, I tried to have another baby as a single mom. I got inseminated with donor sperm and became pregnant, but I miscarried. I'd had many miscarriages prior to having my son, and I realized that I could no longer afford to abuse my body and finances the way I did to get my first and only child. But I'd always thought we were meant to be part of a bigger family: more kids, another adult, a couple of dogs—or at least a cat. Instead, it was just the two of us and a leopard gecko named Michael Jordan. I was ready to consider adopting. I began to imagine that it would be nice to adopt a girl. But there was something else: I was lonely.

When Raphael was in the first grade, I told him that a woman can be in love with a woman and a man can be in love with a man—and that I was gay. Like most boys in first grade, Raphael preferred the company of other boys; he loved the idea that he and his best friend could get married someday. However, he insisted that I wasn't really a lesbian since I didn't have a girlfriend. So I stopped shopping around for sperm and began searching dating sites for a woman.

A year later, when I told Raphael that my friend had become my girlfriend, he was thrilled. He couldn't wait to announce this to the world, beginning with my mom. "Hey Gaga, did you know my mom is a lesbian?"

"Well, I guess I did hear something like that," she told him. He proceeded to spread the happy news to all the guests at a large family gathering. Raphael had already met my girlfriend's daughter, who was the same age as him, and we all got along like a chorus of a lesbian "We Are the World," Jewish, Cuban, Mexican, African-American between us.

"My mom is getting married, and I'm going to have another mom and a sister," Raphael announced to his best friend on an after-school trip in second grade.

"No, you're not," the boy said. "Women can't marry women. She must be marrying a man!" His friend was indignant. When the argument became heated, they deferred to the van driver, who told them that although two women could fall in love, they couldn't, in fact, get married.

In pursuit of a more progressive education for my son, I transferred him to a charter school in Altadena, largely African American and Latino, with more nontraditional families and biracial kids, like Raphael. There, a student told Raphael, "You're not really Black—look in the mirror." Suddenly, my son wanted more than anything to be accepted by a small group of African-American kids whose families were evangelical and vehemently anti-gay. But when Raphael eagerly told them about his "rainbow" family, his classmates were not accepting.

His fourth-grade classmate wagged her finger and shook her head. "What you're doing at home is *your* business, but you can't be bringing that two-mamas stuff here to school!"

That was the same year Raphael started to become aware of contradictions and hypocrisy outside of school. He asked, "If Senator Kerry supports gay people, why is he against gay marriage?"

The parents of an adopted child suggested that the school present the movie *That's a Family*, a sweet film depicting all kinds of parents: single, adoptive, interracial, and, of course, same-sex. A small but vocal minority of parents rallied to stop the screening of the film, and in some misguided show of cultural sensitivity, the administration canceled it. Raphael said, "Mom, it's not the kids. It's what their parents are telling them."

A class from Pitzer College made a documentary about our embattled progressive charter school and the difficulty it was having trying to address homophobia head-on. Raphael had become increasingly aware that not everyone appreciated his blended LGBT family, even though many of his classmates did not live with their traditional nuclear families due to circumstances such as divorce, addiction, or incarceration. But he asked me to let it go so he could just fade into the fray as best he could.

Raphael decided to start remaining quiet about his home situation whenever possible. My girlfriend and I got married in Canada, a public acknowledgement of the blending of our families. The wedding was an important statement to our children—welcoming each of them into our new, combined family unit. We had a family honeymoon on Rosie's Cruise, a boat full of other gay couples and their kids. Raphael said it was a relief to be in a place where he did not have to explain his family.

In a pre-Cosby-scandal world, Raphael wished nothing more than to live in a family like the Huxtables with full siblings and two married, middle-class African-American parents. He struggled in school and in sports and wanted to be like his Black classmates, who played football, got good grades, and lived in "intact" heterosexual families. Being a disorganized, dreamy, awkward Jewish and African American boy with a stepsister and a lesbian mother and stepmom did not win him any points. And a couple years down the line, unfortunately, our blended family unblended.

About five years later, as reflected in the Supreme Court's decision June 26, 2013, the majority of Americans had shifted toward support of same-sex marriage. In that time, Raphael had grown from a self-conscious preteen to a seventeen year old who called himself an Afro-Jew and was at ease with having a lesbian mother.

By 2013, Raphael had posted as his Facebook status, "Don't hide behind the Constitution or the Bible. If you're against gay marriage, just be honest. Put a scarlet 'H' on your shirt and say 'I'm a homophobe!'" A short debate followed among his friends, with the majority liking his post.

When he was younger, the message Raphael heard in his school was that having a lesbian mom was worse than being sold for crack by a straight mom. And society's disapproval was echoed in the laws that discriminated against gay marriage.

But it would also have been illegal for me to marry Raphael's father prior to 1967, when the US Supreme Court unanimously ruled that state bans on interracial marriage violated the Constitution.

In his senior year of high school, Raphael said, "Mom, I'm pretty sure I'm 90% straight." He went on to say that if Ryan Gosling came around, though, he'd be all in. "I can just imagine his strong, muscular arms wrapped around me," he explained. Then he posted this on Facebook. Responses from other boys were mostly rude comments and derogatory terms for homosexuals, but his female friends posted that those guys just weren't as evolved as Raphael. Many young people today seem to embrace the idea of sexual fluidity a lot better than my generation did. I didn't identify as bisexual. Instead, I used to say I was a lesbian in a series of straight relationships.

I recently got married for the third (and hopefully last) time. My wife is in the Coast Guard, but she had left because of "Don't Ask, Don't Tell" when someone was close to telling on *her*. The trauma of secrecy—and always watching her back—hasn't entirely left her, but she rejoined the Coast Guard after DADT was repealed, and she got through boot camp for the second time in her late thirties.

We got married at San Francisco City Hall. Brides and grooms, brides and brides, and grooms and grooms spread out throughout the gorgeous Beaux-Arts building. A few weeks later, we celebrated again at my mom's assisted-living facility. Residents asked a few questions about where the groom was, but most of them were at ease with the two of us.

It seems so long ago that my son's young classmate told him to leave his "two moms" stuff at home. And DADT has been history since 2010. But today I read an essay by a high school student whose family would not accept her attraction to other girls. And we all know that racism didn't disappear with the striking down of the laws against interracial marriage.

Raphael's challenging journey growing up, often feeling he and his family didn't fit in, has provided him with a unique blend of optimism and gritty reality that exceeds my own at times. And so my son is now able to embrace a far more expansive possibility of authentic love, unfettered by fear or intolerance.

My son posted a family wedding photo of us on Facebook. He wrote, "I love these two beautiful ladies! I would only be so lucky to find love close to what you two share."

Wife

BY AMELIA SAUTER

LEAH HAS CANCER.

I arrive at her hospital-room door the same time she does, her on a gurney, me on foot. She opens her eyes and looks at me as they wheel her in. *How did it go?* she asks me. *Hey baby*, I say.

The two nurses, a man and woman who both look like teenagers, detangle her IV lines as they get ready to lift her to the bed. Tubes are coming out of her arm and drains are dangling and peeking out from under her gown. *When can I get out of here?* she whispers hoarsely. *As soon as you can pee and walk*, says the woman. *I'll walk to the bed now*, says Leah. They help her sit up on the gurney, and she wobbles to the bed, almost tipping over from the lingering effects of the anesthesia. The nurses spot her, and she makes it. I continue to stand to the side like a shadow as the nurses help her lie down and put compression sleeves on her legs to prevent blood clots. *I don't like how that feels*, says Leah. They ignore her.

We have to ask you admission questions, they say. Leah is having a hard time holding her eyes open. *Have you fallen recently? No. Do you have a religious affiliation? Definitely not. Are you being abused at home?* She glances at me and we both giggle despite ourselves. She knows not to joke. *No,* she says. *Do you have any open skin ulcers? No.* They apologize for having to "check her bottom" and she moans as they roll her from side to side to look at her butt for bedsores. I think they should have thought of that while she was standing up and her gown was gaping open. *What's your pain on a scale of one to ten? Three. Do you want anything for pain or nausea? No. Here's your call bell if you need anything,* they say.

We are alone. *How did it go?* Leah says again. I don't speak. She puts her hand up to her chest and feels the bandaged flat spot where her left breast was a few hours earlier. She starts to cry. I take her hand. She says, *What did the surgeon say?*

We both know what she is asking. I had no idea that I would be the one to have to tell her. But I am the only one here. I am her wife. *They found cancer in your lymph nodes,* I say. She cries harder. I can't hold her without hurting her so I kiss every part of her face: her forehead, her cheeks, her chin, her nose, and I run my hand over her hair. *I'm so sorry,* I say. *I love you so much. I'm so sorry.* She says, *I need to be alone.*

My mother is waiting for me in the hallway. She has become my best friend these past three weeks. She hugs me, and now it is my turn to cry.

I spend the night with Leah in her hospital room. To my surprise, it is a huge, private room in a new wing. If this was a hotel room, I'd be thrilled: two big closets, a marble sink, recessed mood lighting, a flatscreen TV, and a newly tiled bathroom. But in the middle of the room, instead of a king-size bed with a puffy white comforter, there is a single hospital bed with its bars up and a pale and sleeping Leah lying on it alone. There is a long dark couch that pulls out into a bed for me. I feel lucky to be her wife so the nurses will allow me to spend the night in the room with her.

I quickly realize how the nurses are the lucky ones. I get up over twenty times in the next seven hours, to help Leah to the bathroom, to respond to the alarm when her compression sleeve line gets pinched, to get her a ginger candy, to adjust her pillows, to request pain meds from the nurse, to help her to the bathroom again, to turn down the heat, to turn up the heat, to take off her socks, to get her another ginger candy, to adjust her pillows again, to let someone know the IV is beeping. The nurses come in every four hours to take her vitals. I sleep for a few minutes here and there.

The surgeon arrives at seven a.m. to reiterate for Leah what he told me over the phone from the operating room at seven p.m. the night before: the cancer is invasive. We are home before noon.

We find the best doctors we can in our region. *Who is your surgeon?* other breast cancer survivors ask Leah. *Dr. Yellin,* she says. *Good,* they say, and nod knowingly. We start daily walks per Dr. Yellin's orders. *Because nothing is wrong with your legs,* he tells Leah. Every day becomes consumed with cancer: Leah healing, and me doing all the planning and execution of appointments and daily life. We are driving an hour and a half to the "big city" where my parents live to avoid our country bumpkin hospital (where Leah says she wouldn't get a sliver removed). We drive back and forth to the city two or three times a week for pretests and posttests and bloodwork and complications and follow-ups. We see breast specialists, surgeons, oncologists, radiologists, a geneticist, a cardiologist. We have to come out as gay to all of them.

Which one of you is Leah? the doctors say as they walk in the room. Some of them shake my hand and ask who I am. The rest of them don't greet me or make eye contact with me. It is assumed I am Leah's sister or her friend or a random person who gave her a ride to the appointment and is tagging along into the exam room.

If Leah was at the doctor's office for a flu shot or a strep test, being ignored might not bother me so much. But the words out of these doctors' mouths include things like, *You'll need six weeks of daily radiation* and *You have to have chemotherapy for eighteen weeks followed by eight more months of targeted therapy* and *You're going to have no immune system and lose all of your hair* and *The side effects include DEATH. Now sign the consent form at the bottom.* Leah starts introducing me as her wife before the doctors open their mouths.

Wife. A label I never thought I'd choose, a wedding I never imagined wanting. But falling for Leah changed everything. When I was twenty-six and gallivanting around the country in my camper truck like a hippie wannabe, I met Leah. She was sweet, soft, outspoken, and daring, everything that the men I had slept with were not. Like the flash of a lightning bolt, I went from A, a hopelessly straight girl who vowed to never marry, to Z, hopelessly in love with a woman that I wanted to be with forever.

It was the 1990s. I was in love and scared and often lonely. We were quietly out of the closet when we could be or when we had to be. We moved in together, vacationed in Provincetown where we could hold hands in public, and dared to ride our motorcycles in pride parades enveloped by the cheering crowds even when it meant our photo could end up on the front page of the newspaper before I was out to my parents (which yes, it did, and no, they didn't see it). We patiently settled into our relationship and impatiently waited for the world to change. When same-sex marriage finally became legal in New York, we got married on a beautiful fall day in the company of our friends and family. We would grow old together, through sickness and in health, and live happily ever after until death do us part.

And bam. Here we are. I have become the caregiver. Death is in the room.

Nothing changed when we first became wives, but now, everything is different. We figured we would have decades before one of us would have to worry about getting out of an armchair without assistance. We are having new conversations. *Good job peeing, Leah!* I say, and *The fluid in your drainage balls is looking pretty good today* and *Don't worry, Honey, I don't mind doing the dishes all the time.* I watch Leah sleep at night to make sure she's breathing and I worry about rolling into her. We try sleeping on opposite sides of the bed so I am not near the wound and the drains, but after over twenty years together, it is like trying to sign your name with the opposite hand: illegible, disorienting, and just plain silly. I give her meds to her with a glass of water when the clock tells me to. I cook three meals a day and obsess about her eating, even if it's just chicken broth. I help her take off the bandage for the first time when she confronts the red, angry scar where her beautiful breast was. I yell at people who hug her when her immune system is flatlined. I jump up to let the elderly dog out so she doesn't have to. I don't sleep enough and I drink way too much coffee. I Google her blood-work results. I do not Google cancer. We do not talk about Death.

Leah takes steroids before each chemotherapy treatment. The steroids keep her from sleeping and make her angry and aggressive. We wonder why the hell athletes would want to take this stuff. She gets a lot done in the three days when she takes the steroids before the subsequent chemo crash. My wife with cancer, with no breast, no hair, working like a maniac. She stacks wood. She tiles the floor in the kitchen for our new restaurant that was supposed to be open by now. She builds a twelve-foot-long dining-room table. She hangs drywall. I call her my huzwife. On an afternoon when the steroids are making her particularly edgy, she helps me decorate cupcakes for the one wholesale account that remains since we closed our previous business. Leah painstakingly places hundreds of sliced almonds on dozens of owl cupcakes, one almond for each feather. *Fuck this bullshit!* she yells as she works. *Fuck!* she is muttering and swearing and gently placing almonds on the buttercream owls. *Fuck!* It would be funny if she didn't have cancer. She will sleep and sleep when the steroids wear off.

Even with the steroids and a hefty dose of Benadryl, she has a severe reaction to the chemo one time while we are at the treatment center. A spasm takes hold in her spine as the chemical infusion drips in through the port in her chest, and she doubles over in pain and can't speak. A flurry of nurses surrounds her immediately. They have seen this before. I am pushed to the side. One takes her blood pressure, another yanks the curtains shut, someone temporarily stops the chemo and increases her fluids, and somebody hooks her up to oxygen. The nurse practitioner is in the room in under two minutes. A minute after that, Leah gets a shot of hydrocortisone, and soon she is sitting up and breathing easily again. I watch it all from the sidelines, helpless and amazed.

I hold it together until I have to go to a store, any store. Leah's forty-eighth birthday is coming up, and even though we don't feel like celebrating, I go to Target to get her a a pair of slippers. I'm fine until I get to the women's clothing section. I see a pair of button up pajamas and think, *I should buy these for Leah since she can't put her arm up over her head after the mastectomy.*

Cancer. The reality strikes my emotions like a dagger. I take a pair off the rack as my eyes well up with tears. I look around. Cancer surrounds me. A robe. She needs a robe since she's is in her pajamas so much. I choose a soft grey one for her as I start to cry. A pillow, one of those body-support pillows—ironically called 'husbands'—that she can lean back on while she's in bed. It's the same color gray as the robe. I am compelled to buy it. As I pile each gift into my arms—I hadn't thought to take a shopping cart on the way in—I realize I am not birthday shopping, I am cancer shopping. Cancer is taking over everything. By the time I remember the slippers I have come in for, I am sobbing and dragging my cancer purchases to the register like Steve Martin in *The Jerk*. (*All I need is this ashtray. And this paddleball game. And this lamp. And this thermos. And this chair.*)

Every shopping list is loaded: Zantac for Leah's stomach, vegetables to sneak into her chicken broth, bottled water because they are working on our water main again and I don't know what's in that brown water that could infect Leah. Paint from Lowes for the commercial kitchen? I worry that we'll never open the new restaurant. Batteries for the lights in the gingerbread house that I entered in a contest? We won't be able to go to the artist reception because the crowd will be a breeding ground for the flu. Warm hats? Cancer. Sorbet? Cancer. Christmas cards? Cancer. I don't remember what it feels like to feel normal.

You're so lucky you're both unemployed right now, people say to us. We don't feel lucky. *You're so lucky they caught it early.*

The doctors do not tell us they caught it early. The visits to them are painfully empty of the reassurances we seek. *It could be worse* is the only reassurance they give us. We ask for numbers and percentages and survival rates, but the big-city doctors won't give them to us. *Those numbers are statistics,* they tell us. *We don't know how they apply to an individual.* Leah asks everyone and they all avoid answering. One doctor finally tells Leah he thinks as many as eight or even nine out of ten women with her type of cancer could remain cancer-free after treatment. *But what if I'm the one it comes back for?* Leah asks. *What if it's already in my brain and I don't know it?* The doctors don't do any scans. *If you have symptoms, we'll talk,* they say. Leah says her joints hurt. When she squats down, she can't get up. Her nose bleeds frequently. She has floaters in her eyes now. She sleeps more than she used to. She wonders if she is still anemic and asks for more blood work. *You worry too much,* they tell her. *So does your wife.*

We keep driving back and forth to the big city. It never snows on a Wednesday for the whole winter that Leah gets weekly chemotherapy. For Christmas, my mother buys us a fresh wreath with a big gold bow for our door. I give Leah a chef's knife, and she gives me a rolling pin. Both of these are for the restaurant that we aren't sure we will ever open. We don't say that out loud. We spend New Year's Eve at home, sleeping.

The seasons pass through the windows of the car. Spring flashes by with green landscapes. We have the hottest summer on record and the air conditioning in the car breaks. We can't afford to fix it so we start driving the truck instead. Suddenly the leaves are changing and Facebook tells me it's our wedding anniversary. A year has already passed since Leah's diagnosis. *You've been together for four years,* Facebook says. It makes me angry. I want to post, *Hey, Facebook! You idiot, it's actually twenty-one years!* But it doesn't matter. Everyone is wishing us a happy anniversary on our Facebook walls and posting happy pictures from our wedding. Two days later it is the anniversary of Leah's mastectomy. The doctors tell her she will be done with chemotherapy next month. They say, *We think the cancer is gone but we can't say for certain. The targeted therapy is still too new.* If Leah had been diagnosed fifteen years ago, her type of aggressive breast cancer would be a death sentence. Today the doctors are hopeful.

But Death has entered the room. He gets closer with every passing season. Leah is going to die. Will she die from cancer? Will she die before me? I don't want to think about that now, about losing my wife, or my wife losing me. We should be celebrating our twenty-one years together, our four years married, but we are exhausted. The invincible dykes on bikes who led the pride parade have become a distant memory. We have become old. Death has entered the room, and once he's here, he doesn't leave again. So we pull up a chair for him, open a bottle of wine, and ask, *Where do we go from here?*

Author's note: Leah's breast cancer was discovered during a routine mammogram in 2015 when she was forty-seven years old. She would like you to please pick up the phone and schedule your annual mammogram right now.

The "Duh" Diaries

BY JOEY SCHULTZ-EZELL

IT WAS THE SPRING OF 2005. WITH CONSIDERABLE EFFORT, I'd spent the previous nine months getting sober. A key part of the twelve-step recovery program I was following insisted that we convince our innermost selves that we are alcoholics.

Small problem. My innermost self and I had never been introduced. And if we had at some point in the past, we certainly were not on speaking terms now. I was forty-one, ending a twenty-five-year relationship—and eighteen-year marriage—with my high-school sweetheart, Robby. I was suddenly a single mother to our two kids, Jessy, twelve, and Jason, eight, and hopelessly addicted to my drug of choice: Miller Lite. (I know. At least it could have been a *good* beer. But that is my truth.)

So the short version of my story: I got single. I got sober. I got gay.

Of course, there's more to it than that. A lot more. And I'll be honest, my journey has predominantly been wonderful—filled mostly with humor, love, self-acceptance, and, now, capped with a happy ending that is really just an amazing beginning.

I'm also very aware that my story is unlike that of the many women who have fought, struggled, screamed, marched, and cried to bring themselves where they are today. So many who have been subjected to so much hate, abuse, rejection, and unspeakable pain. And I am deeply and sincerely indebted to those brave women and men.

In May of 2004, Massachusetts became the first U.S. state to legally recognize same-sex marriage. I figured out I was gay almost exactly one year after that historic milestone in New England. And while the path from then to last summer's glorious Supreme Court ruling was not always direct and has included hate-fueled setbacks and too-long stretches of inertia, I confess and admit to riding a wave that I had nothing to do with setting in motion.

After being sober for nine months, for the first time in my life, I was focused on trying to figure out what I wanted. What I liked. What I needed—in work, in life, in relationships. And I had no idea. I was completely clueless.

But clearly something was changing, awakening. Suddenly, women whom I deemed "obviously gay" were paying attention to me. Flirting? Even more surprising, *with me?* I liked it. A lot.

This new awareness started at a recovery weekend in the Ozark Mountains of Arkansas. One woman told me she loved my shirt and smiled at me in a way that made me blush. I was invited to coffee with another woman, and again I blushed as I made up some excuse to back out. And finally, a woman asked me for my phone number so we could stay in touch, following that up with, "Do you have a partner?"

The people who were with me also noticed the attention I was getting and found it all pretty amusing. "It's gotta be the hair," became the inside joke of that three-day weekend.

Ah, the hair. My hair.

Since turning 30, I had begun to get my hair cut in what can only be described as a butch style. Shaved on the sides and short and spiky on the top.

I first cut it that way to get back at my mother, who'd kept me in straight blonde tresses that were so long, I sat on them throughout my childhood. I had been a devout tomboy all my life, and the battles with my mother over my hair and clothes had been many and epic.

But now my hair was short, and I wore the jeans and baggy flannel shirts I'd always wanted to wear. For the next ten years, there were plenty of people who assumed I was gay, but I would always laugh it off and correct them right away.

"Oh, no," I'd say with firm conviction. "I just like it that way. It's simple and easy to take care of. Besides, I'm happily married to a man and have two kids. Straight as they come."

My hair knew I was gay before I did.

So now I'm noticing women noticing me. And I'm noticing them. And I have no idea what to do with the confusing feelings and thoughts running around in my head. Part of the difficulty came from the fact that I had never even been attracted to a woman, at least consciously, and I had never had any kind of a sexual experience with any woman.

None. No college experimenting. No drunken interludes with any of the dozens of gay women with whom I played sports; no dalliances with either of two very close gay friends.

Looking back, that's hard for even me to believe. But it's the truth. I'm pretty sure it had everything to do with the fact that my boyfriend-turned-fiancé-turned-husband and I had simply grown up together. We'd been together from age fifteen to forty, and in all that time, I'd never cheated on him—with a man or woman—and had never really been inclined to do so. (A degree of loyalty I painfully discovered later he did not share.)

I am also not one of those women who have fought and

suppressed natural urges their entire lives before finally coming to a point of strength, or desperation, about their sexuality.

But now I knew that something was different. So I went to my therapist with the information first.

In a halting, shaky voice tinged with both excitement and terror, I tried to explain what was going on. And this beautiful, insightful woman who had already saved my life in myriad ways (and on whom I developed a complete crush, of course) listened quietly and only interjected when I paused before actually saying what I wanted to.

"You're doing great," she said softly. "Go on."

So I did. I told her I was attracted to women. That I thought I might be gay. And I cried. Tears of joy. Not shame. Not confusion. Just joy.

"What do I do now?" I asked, sure she had a distinct path for me to follow.

"I'm not sure."

Excuse me?

She went on to explain that it was not unusual at all for women at my age and stage in life to finally figure out they are gay. She said that most often, they've found themselves attracted to a certain woman. Or had a sexual experience that caught them by surprise and opened up new feelings inside. I had neither of those situations going on.

So what now?

"I'm not sure what to tell you."

Her usual suggestion, she explained, might be for me to go to gay bars and pay attention to how I felt and what kind of women interested me. The problem with that idea, of course, is that *any* bar is an unsafe setting for a newly sober woman—let alone one where I was consciously exploring my sexuality.

Then she told me about a support group a colleague of hers led. And I swear it was called something like The Middle-

Aged, Newly Divorced Moms Who Think They Might Be Gay Group. Seriously. I looked them up online and discovered they were hosting a cookout at a park very near my house that next weekend.

I drove to the park and circled past the cookout no less than six times before finally turning into the lot and parking a safe distance away. They were impossible to miss with several grills fired up, and a raucous volleyball game going on—and a GIANT rainbow flag. They were clearly having fun, and I was immediately drawn to their energy. Then I looked closer.

There were coolers everywhere. And on every picnic table, there were long-neck, brown bottles. Even from that distance, I could recognize the Miller Lite and Bud Light labels.

I almost joined them. But I was certain that I, already uncomfortable and with no accountability, would never be able to resist the first time someone said, "Can I get you a beer?" And as I had used up my life-time supply of cereal malt beverages, that was simply not an option.

So I embarked on a coming-out tour.

I told my sponsor. My closest recovery friend. My recovery roommate. That woman from my group who had moved to Arizona and who I just *knew* was gay. My best friend since childhood. I couldn't tell people quickly enough; I was trying to say the truth as often as possible so it didn't slip away from me.

And as each and every declaration drew near, I got the same anxiety, the same nervous excitement, the same need to rehearse the entire scripted conversation in my head. I felt certain I knew how each of them would react to the "wow" bomb I was about to drop in their lap.

Not so much.

Almost without exception, the unanimous response to the sharing of my mind-blowing, fundamental truth?

"Duh."

At first, each conversation brought huge relief. Eventually, it just got old.

"I was hoping you'd figured that out," my recovery sponsor said.

"I thought that was what you were going to say," my closest recovery friend admitted.

"I've always kind of thought you might be gay," my best friend confessed.

Duh. Duh. And duh. I couldn't decide whether to be relieved or pissed off.

So then I told my roommate, the young woman who was one month ahead of me in sobriety and renting my basement with her boyfriend. Her response? "Yeah."

Or at least that was her initial reaction. It was closely followed with, "I'm sure I've told you that I consider myself bisexual."

No. I am positively certain you have not mentioned that fact. Things suddenly got very interesting.

Would I like to kiss her?

I completely surprised myself by saying yes.

And so I kissed her.

It was incredible. Truly. Such soft, full lips. So gentle. No probing, aggressive tongue. No overtly sexual overtones. Just sensuous. Pleasurable. Warm. Inviting.

"How was that?" she asked.

"Nice," I stammered.

After one more passionate kiss in the kitchen, our flirtation was over, but there were no longer any doubts. I liked girls. And I really liked kissing girls.

Then there was the woman who had moved to Arizona. Given that she was 1,366 miles away, she seemed like a completely safe option to explore all these new-found feelings with.

Weeks of emails and hours-long phone calls followed, fairly innocent at the beginning and progressing into something resembling phone sex. Since she was also in recovery, she would have nothing to do with having a real relationship with me until I had a full year of sobriety.

Once I did, I made plans to treat myself to a trip to Colorado. I invited her to meet me there—in the same place I consumed my last beer—to celebrate my new life.

The four-day weekend started with a long, wonderful, very public kiss at the airport in Denver. An even deeper kiss just inside the hotel-room door, where I was grateful for the wall's support, because my knees were complete jelly. And then a conjoined stumble around the corner to the bed.

I had imagined I would be shy. Or nervous. Or at least polite. I wasn't. We rolled around on the bed, trying to get each other's clothes off, and after she had struggled for what seemed like an eternity with the belt on my pants, she swears to this day I said, "These pants have got to go," and I removed them myself.

Being intimate with a woman was so comfortable. Second nature. I knew what felt good. I had all the same parts. And there was so much tenderness and passion and connection, right from the very beginning.

We spent the next three days in the mountains. Seeing beautiful sights, eating great food, and having incredible sex. Lots of it. As the trip drew to a close, I asked, like some twelve-year-old boy, if she would be my girlfriend.

"What does that mean to you?" she asked. I had no idea. But I did know that I didn't want to see anyone else—and I didn't want her to, either. We at least agreed on that.

She flew to Kansas City two weeks later for a visit. I flew to Phoenix and met her family. She flew back to Kansas City and, on that trip, met my kids, although to them she was introduced only as a friend from Arizona.

As that visit was drawing to a close, I was lying face down on the bed, and she was lying on my back. I asked if she would consider moving back to Kansas City.

"My lease is up in Arizona next month."

Yes.

We agreed she would move back. To my house. And now I had other people to tell.

My parents' reaction stunned me. I was completely unprepared for instantaneous acceptance. At one point, my dad had been one of the most homophobic people in my life. When my oldest cousin died of AIDS, he began to change, but I had no idea how much.

My mother, with the exception of asking me repeatedly if I had ever been with a girl before (*Not Amy? Sue? Cindy? Tina?* Mom, no one. Really.), was also amazingly supportive. My father went so far as to say that he had told my mother that he knew what I was coming to tell them.

Holy hell, even my ex-husband seemed unsurprised. "I always thought you were kind of into girls," he said.

What? A quarter of a century together? A relatively healthy sex life? Never been with a woman? How could his response be nothing more than "duh"?

And there was no way I was going to have my "friend from Arizona" move in without my children understanding the nature of our relationship.

I started with Jessy, then twelve.

"I kind of figured it out, Mom," she said. "I mean, you talk on the phone like two hours every night and you've flown all over to see each other."

But Jason was only eight. And he remains the only "non-duh" response I ever received to my big news. Once I explained that I'd realized I was attracted to women and that I had a girlfriend ("The lady from Arizona?" he asked), there was about a fifteen-second pause. And then he burst into tears.

Huge sobs wracked his little body. There were actual snot bubbles.

Decidedly not a "duh."

Once I calmed him down enough to speak, I asked if he knew what was upsetting him so much.

"The k-k-kids will all m-m-make fun of me," he said.

"We won't tell them."

"We can do that?" he said, beginning to relax.

"Of course."

"Oh. Okay. Then that's okay."

I told him he would probably think of questions later, and he should feel safe to ask as many as he wanted. He said he wanted to be left alone.

I heard a small, timid tap at my door about twenty minutes later.

"Mom, does this mean you hate men?"

"No. I'm just not attracted to men. I'm attracted to women. It's called being a homosexual, which means I'm attracted to someone the same sex as me." He had been studying Latin roots to words, so this explanation made perfect sense to him.

My relationship with Arizona lasted eight years. Parts of it were amazing and parts were not. I continued to grow and get stronger and develop a healthier sense of what I wanted and needed in a relationship. I became secure enough to ask for and expect those changes. But when counseling and talking and fighting couldn't fix it, I made a decision to end it.

And then, almost immediately, I fell in love with Lauren. Really in love. You have to love yourself first to do that, and I did.

Everything about this new relationship was "too much, too soon, too fast." And we both knew it. But our response to those warnings eventually became "too bad."

Lauren also has a son and daughter, and together our kids range in age from twenty to twenty-five. At one point, they all lived here with us and we called ourselves the "Gaydy Bunch." We also had six cats, three dogs, four turtles, and couple of "spare boys" along the way (friends of my son, who came to stay "for just a couple of weeks" and left years later). Our home is filled with recovery and love and second chances.

On September 4, 2016, Lauren and I were married. Our kids stood with us, our parents sat in the front row and hundreds of our closest friends and family joined us to celebrate.

That day. This life. All of it. This is the precious gift given us by the hard-fought battles of the tens of thousands who came before and for whom I am eternally grateful.

Because after getting engaged, Lauren and I had agreed that we didn't want to travel to Hawaii or Canada or even nearby Iowa to *get* married. We wanted to *be* married. And that's what last summer's Supreme Court ruling provided us. Married. Legally. In Kansas, of all places. And there is nothing—absolutely nothing—"duh" about that.

Swept Away

BY EMILY J. SMITH

AT DINNER WE TALK ABOUT TINDER. MY FRIENDS AND I are always talking about Tinder. It's our teenage dream come true, twenty years later: knowing when someone you like likes you back. It's addicting, like a slot machine of confidence. We're racking up chips and swiping our way toward someone we can spend time with because an "other half" will make us whole, and that half must be in there somewhere if we just swipe fast enough.

I'm swiping right in all the right places, matches are being made. But when I think about waking up next to the people on my tiny screen—the man with a dark beard who's *a fan of witty banter,* or the skinny tall one who *likes beer and board games*—I panic. My stomach drops like I'm waiting to give a speech, preparing every inch of my body for a performance.

My body is tired of performing. My twenty-something self was shards of a million other people's selves. Paul with his records and Peter with his philosophy. Mike and his hikes, John and *The Wire.* All of them and David Foster Wallace. Some girls like eyes, others go for height, I wanted interests. I wanted to make them mine, leech onto these men and suck the passions right out of them. I obsessed over Yo La Tengo and Immanuel Kant, learned guitar and how to cook, because those pursuits were not just preapproved, they were purposeful. If I was interested in these men's interests, then by some property or another, I, too, would be interesting to these men.

It's not that I silenced my own interests—I wasn't aware of their existence. I wasn't aware of their lack of existence, either. Maybe I *did* like Yo La Tengo, hiking wasn't *that* boring, but the line between what I wanted and what they wanted me to be was so thin and blurry it was impossible to discern. I was a reflection of men's desires and it felt like enough; more than enough, it felt like the point. Following their lead made sense—it had come in handy for so long.

To fit in, my voice shrank from curious, thoughtful comments to cheerful confirmations. My interests shrank from sketching and music and gadgets, to just gadgets, then watching boys play with gadgets.

And my body shrank. I stopped eating. I think I resented my body. I think I wanted to fit in. The more I learned, the more it seemed that a woman's body existed for others. A child, and a man, could run fast, climb high, and move easily. As a woman, I had no use for my breasts or my curves. My period was unbearable. And it gave me a clear, measurable target. Beauty standards were clear: thinner was better. If that was the goal, I could achieve it. I clung to this new, measurable standard because its execution was entirely under my control. I was too committed to notice that its definition had nothing to do with me. That this standard of success stood in the face of every one of my natural desires.

I forced my body back, away from the woman it had grown into and reversed it into a pile of sharp, sexless edges. I lost my period and much of my hair, neither of which ever returned. My veins were visible on every part of me, but hidden under oversized

Old Navy fleeces and baggy boyfriend jeans. I became unburdened by size or shape. I wanted to prove that I didn't need my body as a woman—that maybe I was better off without it.

I wish I could use this space to describe one big, dramatic event that allowed me to stop caring, to sweep the shards of other people away and fill up with my own chunky pieces of self, but there was no event. There was no start and no end, just a slow layering of my own needs. I built habits and routines that allowed me to grow, to survive, within the safety of my own carefully constructed terms. With no one watching, I let myself eat meals without counting. I bought clothes that fit my body instead of fitting my body into clothes. I learned to enjoy what I wanted. I learned what wanting even meant. My routines served as padding between who I was and who they wanted me to be.

I built walls. Walls protected me from the careless men who judged the curl in my hair or the fit of my jeans. Men who didn't want me to worry, wanted me to drink their beers and eat their burgers and laugh, but still be small, so small. Men who wanted me to care about something passionately, but didn't care to hear what I cared about.

Walls helped. I needed walls.

I move across the country because what I want is to be back home in New York. It feels right, the changing seasons, the direct conversation, my parents just a train ride away. I find an apartment, start a new job. I meet new friends because I have no old friends here.

I don't realize it's happening, because it hasn't happened in years, but the new friend across from me makes every second feel better than my seconds alone. She listens. She smiles. She talks with me, not at me. I am to her what she is to me: an interesting person. She looks at me curiously, wanting more than the simple validation of her words. I want her face close to mine. I want her body close to mine.

Again I panic, but not like I'm giving a performance. More like I'm jumping off a cliff.

Anxiety takes over as I become lost in an avalanche of questions. The obvious: How does this work with a woman? I'm thirty-five, is it even worth it? Does she feel it too? How do I even tell? The less obvious: What if she sees that I eat the same meal every night because my anorexia still stalks my every move? What if I reveal myself as the most boring person in the world? Someone who wants to spend Saturdays sleeping and writing and sitting silently for hours? What if I don't have time to do my run every day because there are other things she wants to do together and I can't say no?

She scoots closer on her stool. Her hand touches mine, softly at first and I don't pull away. Her fingers curl around mine on the sticky wooden bar.

As she speaks, I see my web of habits as a different kind of padding. The padding you pile into a box to keep a prize safe. Padding that's both necessary and useless depending on when and how you use it; indispensable until you get where you need to be, and then it's just in the way, a messy pile of similar scraps. The more valued the prize, the denser the padding, the more there is to sweep away once you arrive.

Strong Like Her

BY STAR McGILL-GOUDEY

"FULL ON BODY TREMORS . . . MY KNEES BECAME SO WEAK I sank into his arms, stars spun in my head until my breath and his breath were one pulsing energy." That is how my friend described kissing a boy. I didn't feel anything like that when I kissed boys.

I was clueless about my own biology, thanks to a sex education consisting of a church-approved stick-figure book and being told how sinful it was to feel what my body was supposed to be feeling if it didn't happen within marriage. In *Top Gun*, when Kelly McGillis walked across the screen, I felt heat wrap across my body and make my brain fuzzy. Meanwhile, my friends felt the same way about Tom Cruise. Back at church on Sundays, I would hear about the evil homosexuals trying to take over the world. I pushed my feelings down. I had no one to talk to.

Satan was calling me in the way my body was coming to life, in the way I felt for women. I knew that unless I could control my body, I was headed into an eternity of pain, and my family would be struck down to teach me lessons. I pleaded and prayed and bargained with God. I prayed to be possessed by a husband, by God, by Jesus, never knowing I was actually free to make my own path.

At twenty-one, I joyfully stood at the front of my ancestral church. I thought I was marrying my best friend, that the feelings of heat and wild abandon for him would come within marriage and that we would live happily ever after. I didn't see how much he was like my father. He joined the military and through our travels, I began to befriend people of all religious beliefs and sexual orientations. I had been taught people of different beliefs were evil, but I liked my new friends. They were great people. Normal. Happy. Even though they were sinners.

Our nomadic lifestyle brought a new awareness that changed my perspective and introduced me to worlds I never imagined. But the real catalyst for change in me was my mother.

My mother's focus had always been on the wants and needs of others, never her own. As years passed, I watched her become despondent—my father was abusive to her and she worked all hours of the day and night to support our family. When I was an adult, she told me that she became so exhausted that she often thought of driving her car across the median of the busy highway—if only she could be certain she wouldn't hurt anyone else in the process.

When she first felt the lump she did nothing. Whatever it was, my mother was prepared to let it take her. Then I told her I was pregnant, and she rushed to the doctor, only to be told she had rapidly growing triple-negative breast cancer. She wanted to fight. She wanted to see her granddaughter grow. But it was too late. She died on my daughter's second birthday after battling cancer with chemo, radiation, mastectomy, and drugs. This woman who cared so much for others did not value her own life. As the church taught her, she was only good because she was an obedient vessel (victim) letting Jesus work through her. She never knew she had anything else but that ancient book of oppression and horrors.

That was the only book she let herself believe. My mother was deeply good and strong, but she never knew it, and she never knew the truth about me.

When she was dying, my queer and atheist friends stood by me, without the judgment and trite words I would hear from family and church friends. My queer and atheist friends held space for me and loved me in a way I had never experienced. Some I had known since childhood, and others were friends I had met online in crunchy mom groups. I had always prayed for them to renounce their sins and be saved, and it was they who were saving me. When Mom died, my last thread to the church had been cut. What I had been taught no longer made sense. My repression was beginning to lift as I journaled and found a new freedom to look at myself openly. Now, anything was possible.

Right around that time, my husband told me about childhood friends of ours: a man and a woman who were now married. She had realized she was bisexual, and they were exploring polyamory. This excited me in a way I never expected. I was thinking about women again, but this time, I was free to do so.

I looked at online profiles, and met a woman for dinner. It was comfortable and sexy all at once. Her eyes held mine as we smiled and blushed a bit. Our hands brushed over the sushi we ordered, and I felt that long-lost heat wrap around me again. My body was coming alive, and I felt like the lights above the booth burned even more brightly because of my pulsating energy. We talked for hours, and then had to return to our husbands and kids. I pressed her close when we said goodnight. It was a chaste hug in public, but I could feel every curve pressed against me, the soft brush of her long hair against my cheek. I wanted to keep holding her.

I went home and bawled. I was overcome with the thought of turning the shower on hot, and scrubbing my body with bleach and a Brillo pad as I wailed, crumpled into the shower floor. In the days that followed, I journaled, prayed to a God I didn't believe in, ran miles until I was exhausted, drank, tried to get her off my mind. It was no use. She haunted me. I realized if I didn't follow this through then I would never be okay again.

Not long after, my husband and I went to our polyamorous friends' house for dinner. It took me an entire evening of wine and hot-tub flirting before I got the nerve to tell the men to go inside for a bit and let me kiss her. She was wearing a bikini and the water was lifting her breasts up so that the moonlight was high-lighting each curve and sway. Her apple-cider-smelling perfume was intoxicating. She was talking to me as she moved closer, about what I don't know—all I could feel was an electric charge between us that made me tremble. I touched her skin, watching my fingers trace lines on her arm and shoulder, watching her breath catch. She was still trying to talk in faltering words as I slid my hands into the hot, bubbling water and around her waist. I could feel her breath on my neck as I pulled her close. My brain froze, the only words I could speak were "Shut up and kiss me," and she dove to my lips, pressing hers hard into mine. I could taste lip gloss, the champagne; could feel her breasts and mine pressed together, her tongue sliding against my lips, my tongue. I could feel how soft and hard she was all at the same time, how I wanted to tumble into that softness. The world set to spinning and we pressed closer.

That first kiss left me with the knowledge of myself and my love of women—and it left me mad drunk with the need for more.

After that, my husband and I decided to try polyamory. I think we saw it as the solution to our problems. It was only fair, right? We read *Opening Up* and hoped to become acquainted with a suitable couple. A very attractive woman contacted me through a secret group on Facebook, after seeing some burlesque photos that I posted. We texted and flirted before we met a week later for dinner.

She had me so turned on before I even left the house; I was intoxicated by her pictures and her unabashedly sexual texts. We went to their house after dinner for drinks and conversation that led to much more on many nights to come. I loved to run my hand through her hair, smell the perfume at the base of her neck, slide my hands across her cheek, across her lip. Loved to hear her speak my name. She had seen and wanted me, that's what I thought. But it turned out she had fallen in love with my husband and he with her. They had been seeing each other before this setup. I was crushed.

Within months, my marriage was over. I began to live my life on my terms. I went to counseling, learned about conscious parenting. I applied for an apartment on campus as a single mom, went to school, and worked part time. When my daughter was with her father, I dated men and women, always being honest about dating others and often being met with far less than honesty in return. After the poly experience with my ex-husband, honesty was the most important thing to me.

I met a singer with red hair and an amazing body. One summer night I watched her on stage. Her eyes burned into me as she sang, and I knew each twist of her hip was for me. After her set, she pressed into me at the bar. Her dress skimmed every curve. I slipped an ice cube out of my drink and pressed it to her throat, slid it down her neck, across her bare shoulder, my hand moving up her thigh. She quivered and pressed farther into me, turned to kiss me, ice dripping over us both. Every eye in the club was watching us. We were safe here. She wasn't out and everywhere else we went, we had to be discreet. A hand on a leg under a table. Stolen kisses in the car. We would talk for hours and meet for lunches; she became my best friend. I wanted more than poly from her. I played with her husband just to have more time with her. Their rules dictated that she never was able to spend time with me alone. But I had inhaled her. She was in my bloodstream. This was breaking my heart, and eventually, I had to let her go.

When I was married, I thought sex would solve everything. Now I had all these sexual experiences ranging from the passionate to tepid, and I was still hollow. Most of the women I dated were bisexual, poly, and married. Some would date me just in the hopes of a threesome, and they only pretended to care. How I felt often did not matter. I knew I needed someone who understood and valued all of me and did not exploit me. I realized that gender didn't matter. I wanted the one who saw my soul and wanted more. The journey companion. My best friend for life. Whose touch ignited me inside and out. Someone honest, someone I could trust. Home. Passion. Fire. Future. Family. I was searching. And with each person I was with, I lost more hope and died a little more within myself.

Oddly enough, I found love when a friend introduced me to her ex-husband. We talked and texted for weeks. I met him for the first time at his home, after getting lost in a cornfield. I pulled up in his driveway and laid eyes on my future husband for the first time. He had light hair, broad shoulders, strong arms, and he carried himself with hypnotizing confidence. My heart quickened and I was too nervous to get out. I waited. He leaned into the window and smiled. Welcomed me to his home. An English mastiff and labs crowded around his feet. I could tell they liked him, respected him, trusted him. He opened my door for me and I found my feet. He looked me up and down and smiled. His blue eyes burned into mine and took my breath. I was home. He blew my mind and my body wide open with more passion, tenderness, love, and respect than I ever knew possible.

I am now happily married to him, and yet I crave women at times. It caused deep guilt for a while. Why couldn't I be normal and monogamous? It was the church creeping in again. It seems it's never completely gone. My husband knew before he met me, and he told me he would never try to change me and make me miserable. I have no desire to sneak around. We have met couples and have had some fun evenings living our mutual fantasies, and I am free to find a girlfriend if I would like. It's hard to find women who are bisexual and who interest me in this very rural conservative region. Very few are out. Many are purely swingers who want sex and casual friends at best. I want more than casual sex. I don't know when or if I will meet another girlfriend. I am okay with that. I am okay with me.

I love myself now. It's been excruciating and exhausting to wade through everything I have been taught, all the abuse, traditions, and expectations that surrounded me, to find who I am. To give up on the ridiculous idea of being normal. Like my mother, I thought about suicide many times, but my daughter kept me going, and I am too much of a fighter to give up. I have walked through nights so deep and dark that every breath cut canyons through my skin and fear ripped at my heels. Arms wrapped tightly around my knees, rocking back and forth and wailing from places I never knew existed inside. I wish I could go back and tell myself and my mother: You will walk through this, dear one. You will find yourself. Never give up. You are not alone.

The Flipping of the Switch

BY M. E. TUDOR

I THINK WATCHING THE 1996 *20/20* INTERVIEW WITH Melissa Etheridge and her partner, Julie Cypher, was what flipped the light switch in my closet. The way the two of them looked at each other made me realize I was missing something. That night, I had the most vivid dream about having sex with another woman, a dream so strong that I woke up wondering where the woman had gone. This, of course, pleased my husband, Kelly, to no end. He had been trying to talk me into having sex with a woman while he watched for almost all thirteen years of our marriage.

At the time, we were living with our two young daughters in Montrose, California, a very small city in the eastern slopes of the Rocky Mountains. I had always tried to be the perfect wife. My parents fought all the time. I hoped that if I did everything my husband asked of me, then I would have a happy life. We'd met as teenagers and married young. We had a lot of happy times, but things had changed. Kelly had changed. He'd always been demanding and sexually driven, but he'd wanted me to do things

I didn't feel comfortable doing. When I didn't do what he wanted, I felt useless and stupid.

A few months later we moved to the much larger city of Colorado Springs, and my husband intensified his demands that I find a woman with whom to have sex. Just about every night he wanted me to tell him about the dream again and describe it. He sent me to a lesbian bar one night to try to pick someone up, but I couldn't stand the thought of asking any of the women in the bar if they would go home with me.

I have to admit that after the dream I was intrigued by the idea. There were several women in the bar that I wouldn't have minded getting to know, but I felt dirty even thinking about asking them to let my husband watch us. When that didn't work, he said that he'd seen personal ads in one of the local papers and he wanted me to answer one of them.

I answered a personal ad placed in a small community paper by a woman looking for a bi-curious woman. I was surprised when the woman (I'll call her Jane) called me. She sounded very nice, and we made arrangements to meet at the park downtown the next day. She was very pretty with long red hair and big blue eyes. I was immediately attracted to her. We talked for over an hour and made arrangements to have dinner that evening. My husband was invited, but he declined, saying he would stay home with our two daughters. The plan was that I would just meet with her and her boyfriend and talk and nothing else.

When I got to the house, she greeted me at the door. Her boyfriend said hello but then left the two of us alone. After a few minutes of polite conversation, she asked me if I wanted to kiss her. I kissed her tentatively, but the fire between us soon ignited and before I knew it we were in her bed. From the moment we kissed, all my fear about not knowing what to do left me. I knew exactly what I wanted to do to her and I did it. It was the most amazing sexual experience, up to that point, in my life. I left their home completely elated and certain we would meet again.

When I returned home, Kelly was waiting for me. I told him that I'd had sex with the woman without him there; that it had just happened. I figured, from the tenor of our conversations, that he would want to hear about it. I thought he would be happy I had sex with her. But he was not. He was furious. That night, we had the worst fight of our marriage. He was certain I'd slept with her and her boyfriend, which I had not. Her boyfriend tried to join us, but I had drawn the line with him because I knew Kelly would be pissed if I slept with him.

Nevertheless, Kelly told me he was going to leave me, and then came back and demanded I tell him if I still loved him. Angry, I said I didn't love him anymore. But after I spoke the words, I realized they were truer than I ever realized. So marked the beginning of two horrible years.

Jane called me a few days later. She and her boyfriend had enjoyed my company and wanted me to come over again. I told her that my husband's feelings about the situation had changed, and that I wouldn't be able to see her. She was very understanding.

Soon after, we moved from Colorado to Kentucky. We weren't there six months before Kelly wanted to move again, to Florida. Kelly was a drywall hanger and finisher. We were constantly going back and forth between living close to family in Indiana and Kentucky, and going where the money was in Florida and Colorado.

Earlier in our marriage, I found moving frequently to be a lot of fun. I'd grown up in a very small town in western Indiana and my parents led boring lives, other than their violent fights. I met Kelly when I was sixteen and he was eighteen. He was very self-assured and had big dreams. I just knew he would take me away from my mundane life in Indiana, and he did. I'd grown up in a home where my father controlled everything, so marrying a man similar to my father hadn't been a huge stretch for me. I have always been mild-mannered and allowed Kelly to rule over me. I thought that was the way it was supposed to be.

Things became more and more strained between my husband and me. The verbal and emotional abuse that had been a constant in our marriage became more vicious. He became rougher and more demanding during sex. He made me feel like I owed it to him because I'd had sex with a woman and he didn't get to watch.

I had worked with Kelly for years hanging drywall and did so again, but this time in Florida, he accused me of checking out other women working on the sites, or stopping to watch women sunbathing in the backyards of the houses. One time, we were walking through Wal-Mart and a particularly pretty woman walked by. I did look. Twice. He turned and looked at the woman and said at the top of his lungs, "You want me to ask her out for you?" The woman and I were both very embarrassed.

By the end of the first year back in Florida, Kelly decided he wanted to move back to Kentucky with his cousins. I was pretty much done with our marriage and seriously considering going to Texas to stay with my sister, but something told me to go to Kentucky with him. At first, I was really sorry I did. I didn't think it was possible, but he became even more abusive, especially sexually. I immediately found a well-paying job in a factory and started making plans to leave him.

I wasn't sure if I could get away from him, but I was determined to try. What made it even more important for me: my daughters. We'd moved so many times that our oldest daughter had been in seven different schools, and they were both having behavioral problems.

Kelly seemed to have picked up on my feelings, and started showing up at home early or not going to work. I also started suspecting he was using hard drugs. He'd always smoked pot and drank some, but there were radical changes in his behavior. I started finding clues around the house. A mirror that looked like it had smudge lines across it. Sandwich bags with white residue in the bathroom trash. Plus he rarely worked but always seemed to have money, which made me suspect he might be dealing. I had to find some relief from his presence, so I signed up to bowl with the local women's league.

One of the women's teams needed a full-time player and I was happy to join them. Kelly insisted I take our two preteen daughters with me when we played.

The first night, I noticed a cute redhead bowling on one of the other teams. My eyes sought her out often. I highly doubted I would meet any gay woman in the small city in which we were living and chastised myself for staring at her. But I found I couldn't stop. I noticed that she had started watching me too.

The night finally came when we were to bowl against the redhead's team. I couldn't believe how nervous I was about meeting her. I assumed my attraction to her was one-sided, but that didn't decrease my anxiety. Her name was Rosa.

She gave me a warm smile when we started bowling. She was strong and confident, and I tried to resist sneaking peeks at her, but it was hard. When she made her first strike, everyone from both teams gave her high fives. I reached out to shake her hand, and was shocked by the electricity I felt pass between us. I looked into her light blue-green eyes and saw she'd felt it too.

We talked a little that night and I introduced her to my two daughters. Everyone on her team was friendly, except the woman who she came in with, who gave me dirty looks. I didn't think much of it at the time, because she had always seemed to be in a sour mood.

Weeks went by, and Rosa and I spoke as we'd pass each other, occasionally running into each other in the restroom (which I timed, perfectly). Finally there came a night when I didn't have my girls and she wasn't with her friend. We were bowling in neighboring lanes and spent the night talking. She told me she was in charge of the tool room at the local woodworking factory, and that she had grown sons. She invited me to McDonald's next to the bowling alley for coffee after we finished. I thought I would lose my mind, because I knew my husband would be pissed off and suspicious if I came home late, but I couldn't pass up this chance to be alone with her.

We sat across from each other and talked even more. She explained that the woman she came with was her girlfriend. Now her dirty looks made sense. She told me that things were bad between them and they fought about her two sons, one who lived with Rosa's mother, and one who lived with Rosa's ex-husband. I told her that I thought my abusive husband was using hard drugs. Before the night was over, she took my hand. We acknowledged our attraction to each other, both of us realizing that there was nothing we could do about it.

Rosa and I talked every chance we got after that, which wasn't as often as I would've liked. I gave her my phone number, and she started calling me at home. I tried to make sure we timed it so my husband wouldn't be home. One time I was on the phone with her when he came in. I knew he was suspicious about our friendship.

Kelly tried to sabotage my success during this time. He hid my keys from me so I would be late to work. He kept me up late. He blew up the motor in my car. I had a couple of coworkers who lived out that way who said they'd give me a ride, but then help came from an unexpected source. My brother-in-law Russell let me borrow his van until I could get another car.

We hadn't been in Kentucky six months when Kelly started talking about moving back to Colorado. He must have sensed I wasn't going with him, but I wasn't going to tell him that. His drug use was becoming more evident, his moods more volatile.

He left right after Thanksgiving to go to Colorado to work and I was so relieved. Life was much more peaceful for my girls and me when he wasn't around. I'd continued putting money away and packing clothes for the girls and me in case we had to leave in a hurry. With him gone, I started packing what I wanted and preparing for the time when the girls and I would leave.

Rosa called more frequently and we talked longer. I knew her girlfriend had to be suspicious. Rosa and I tried to stay in the platonic friendship zone, even though I knew I was falling in love with her.

My husband came back a few days before Christmas and the next two weeks were the worst of my life. We fought constantly. He didn't accuse me of fooling around (without his consent), because he knew I didn't believe in that, but he forbade me to talk to Rosa. But I still did—just not when he was around.

He left to go back to Colorado on New Year's Day, and I kissed him good-bye, knowing it would be the last time I did so. I was done. I wasn't going to continue living this vagabond life, dragging my girls from school to school, and I wasn't going to give up another good job, especially when I didn't want to be with him anymore. I wanted to be with Rosa, but that wasn't the only reason why I was going to end my marriage. I was ending it because I'd had forty-five addresses in fifteen years. Because I was tired of "Bitch" being my pet name, and of being used and degraded. I didn't know at this point if Rosa would even leave her girlfriend. Yes, our bond was strong, but they'd been together for a long time.

A few days after my husband left, Rosa called me and said she needed to see me. I asked her to come out to my house. I was a nervous wreck. I got out a bottle of wine, fed the girls, and made sure they would be ready to go watch TV so Rosa and I could talk.

When she arrived, I greeted her on the back porch of the house. She gave me a long, lingering hug. We went inside and visited with the girls and my dog before sending the girls upstairs to their rooms. The energy between us was palpable. She told me that she'd broken up with her girlfriend and moved to her mother's house. We talked for a few minutes longer, and then I told her I had something to show her in my bedroom. I wanted to show her my new earrings—and get her alone so I could kiss her, which is what I did.

The kiss was amazing. For the first time in my life I actually felt my knees go weak. We continued to kiss and touch each other until we came to our senses and realized that I had kids in the house. I was still married, and I wasn't a cheater. Rosa spent the night. As much as we both wanted each other, we did nothing more than sleep curled up together.

My husband called just about every night wanting to have phone sex. It was hard to keep up pretenses. By the middle of January I couldn't continue, so I told him I wanted a divorce. He was furious. We had a huge fight over the phone. He accused me of leaving him for someone else, and I denied it. For several months, he'd call repeatedly, accusing me over and over again until finally I screamed, "This is all your fault! If you hadn't wanted me to have sex with another woman, I would never have known that I was gay!" I went off about several other reasons why I was leaving that were his fault, like his drug use and talking to me like a dog. Afterwards, I felt . . . *good*.

The day after I told Kelly I wanted a divorce, Russell sat me down and told me about everything Kelly had been doing behind my back for years. He told me about the women and the drugs. I'd never felt so foolish.

Now it's been more than eighteen years since Rosa and I first met, and we are still together.

I have no doubts about my sexuality. I believe I have always been gay and just didn't understand why I always wanted to hang out with the girl basketball star or the married friend who wanted to take me to the movies. Or the complete infatuation I had with my best friend all through high school. But I'm glad I didn't know I was gay before I did. If I had, I probably would never have found my soul mate and the love of my life.

Teaching Out

BY SUSAN WHITE

THE YEAR 1999 MEANS MORE TO ME THAN PRINCE'S ICONIC party song. This was the year that my three fundamentals of life—marriage, job, and home—exploded.

In early October 1999, I lived in a dormitory on a boarding-school campus in North Carolina with my rescue dog, Zora. I was teaching English, coaching cross-country, serving as dorm mother, and having an affair with Leslie, my running partner—who happened to be married to our Admissions Director, who was good friends with Headmaster Parsons. My husband of seven years had moved out the previous spring after my second affair with a woman. My one-week fling with a sexy, female academic two years earlier he had chalked up to my being "curious" or "intellectually smitten," which I went along with because, quite frankly, I'd hoped he was right. But now it was clear. I was gay.

Leslie, a mother of three, had managed to hide the affair. But as the air chilled, our infatuation announced itself like the red maple leaves on the quaint, hilly campus.

My fall went down like this: Leslie's husband told the

headmaster about our affair, and he gave me four hours to get off the campus after calling me a sinner and homewrecker and telling me I was sick—with the caveat that after counseling, I could perhaps teach again; Zora and I moved into a house inhabited by three other queer adults (two females and a male); I called my parents to tell them that I was not only separated from James, but that I had been fired, and I was gay. "Oh thank God," my father said. "I thought you were going to tell us you were an alcoholic."

I am fortunate, unlike some others. A gay friend of mine from graduate school had been chased out of his home by his gun-wielding mother. But my parents' love for me was not shaken. Still, even with family support, I reeled through the days—concussed from the fall from my previous life. How was I, a thirty year old with a masters in English, who had been fired a few months into a school year, going to find a job? And now I was a lesbian, too. Anytime I left my new house, I feared contact with someone who knew the dirty details of my scandal.

I was not a victim; I had lied to and betrayed a man who was once my best friend, and I had watched Leslie's husband cry for himself and his children. Leslie and I clung to each other in the center of fiery judgment.

After I was fired, I threw as much as I could away. I should have returned the headmaster's card praising my work and skills, which he'd written a month before he fired and damned me. But I didn't. Instead, I chose to believe him: that I would never teach again without counseling, and I heaved my file cabinet full of teaching materials and lesson plans to the bottom of a deep, metal receptacle at the dump.

I paid a lawyer to procure a letter of recommendation from the Dean of Faculty that honestly reflected my performance as a teacher and coach. And, in exchange for my signed agreement not to sue, the school agreed to respond to all inquiries that I had resigned for personal reasons.

By the end of October, I was tutoring at the Sylvan Learning Center. I did not actually teach; in this factory of daycare tutoring, I followed prescribed lessons attached to color-coded, numbered texts. As instructed, I doled out prizes for participation and completion. I was not a teacher; I was a Pez dispenser. At first, I felt relieved to not have to prepare motivating, substantial lessons and grade a mountain of writing. But within a few weeks, I longed to be responsible for designing ways to help young people grow as people, readers, writers, and communicators—as navigators of life and relationships. But I didn't see how I could do that from the camp of the ostracized literary characters I had studied with students: Hawthorne's Hester Prynn, Baldwin's David, Woolf's Rhonda, McCullers's Miss Amelia.

Before long, I was promoted to administering and scoring IQ tests, and I found the process mildly interesting. One day I sat in the testing center, waiting to test a recruit for the police force, and in walked my former headmaster's wife. She didn't see me as she asked the receptionist what time her husband's test would be over. The man who called me sinful and sick was taking a theology test.

As she settled into one of the brown, plastic chairs, our eyes met. She looked down, fiddled with her bracelet, then exited the room. After I administered the IQ test, I left for my lunch break and saw her hiding in her car, talking on her cell phone.

When I crossed paths with ex-colleagues, we either pretended not to see each other, or we spoke in choppy generalities with flushed faces. I wrote letters to the teachers I considered to be friends, but they did not respond. I had to let those people go.

Then, as November ended, a family friend who had moved to Asheville told me something that would reroute my life: The rival day school needed a qualified, experienced person to teach eighth-grade English for a semester. She urged me to apply.

Even though I knew serious barriers lay between me and the teaching job at the renowned day school, something inside me said to leap from deadening stability toward my calling. I declined my boss's promotion at the learning center and desperately hoped my application to the day school would put me back in a classroom—even if it was just for a semester. I knew the boarding-school overseers had signed an agreement to never discuss the details of my departure, but gossip is a raging fire in small towns, and a scant forest separated these two schools. The red-faced theologian-to-be headmaster haunted me.

I was in the shower when one of my housemates ran into the bathroom with the portable phone because Brenda Bock, the middle-school principal, was on the line. As I sat on the closed toilet lid, shampoo running into my eyes, Brenda told me I was one of the three applicants she would like to interview. My whole body buzzed with gratitude as she mentioned over fifty people had applied for the position.

I have only been as nervous as I was during that interview a few times in my life. Though I was convinced I offered what they needed, each time Principal Bock paused, I was positive she was about to ask me if it was true I was gay and had had an affair with a mother of three. After our tour of the school, she brought me back to her office and said, "I do not need all the details, but I am wondering why you chose to leave your last teaching job in the fall." My adrenaline surged as I explained, "I had a major personal conflict." Then I said too much. "My leaving was due to an affair; it had nothing to do with the quality of my teaching or coaching."

When I got home, I grabbed Zora and ran up and down the hills of our neighborhood, replaying the explanation I gave for leaving my last school. I stopped. Gasped. Held my hands up to my mouth. Did I make it sound like I had an affair with a student? Oh my God. What had I done? I couldn't run home fast enough to call the principal.

I was breathing hard when I asked the secretary to connect me to the principal. She told me Brenda Bock was in a meeting, so she put me through to her voicemail. Because I could not wait another second to tell her I had *not* had an affair with a student, I left a rambling, emotional message telling her what I worried she *might have thought*—and that I had, in fact, had an affair with an adult on the campus. Though my message was raw and inarticulate, I was relieved to have blurted out the clarification.

The next day, the principal called me and offered me the job. She laughed about my message and hinted that she had heard the gist of my personal conflict from her friends who worked at my old school. And then she struck a serious tone: "I want you to know you are starting with a blank slate here. But this is a conservative school, and you should not share the details of your personal life."

So when Leslie and her three children popped in to visit me in my classroom, I was horrified and shooed them away as fast as possible. A couple days later, I heard a male science teacher gravely telling Brenda the rumor he heard about me. That night, I barely slept, and for weeks I shied away from my colleagues. At music concerts, I rebuffed Leslie's open signs of affection for fear students' parents were near.

But in the classroom I was on fire. The students were shocked by their increased work and my high expectations after enjoying the previous teacher's easy-going disposition and less rigorous curriculum.

We tackled short stories by Chekhov, Baldwin, Hemingway, Cisneros, Updike, O'Connor, and Alexie. We read novels, poems, and essays that zinged questions and opinions of war, love, family, and identity around our discussion circle. We pushed back the tables and performed Shakespeare's satirical play of the asses we become under the spell of love. We grabbed onto the thin branches of truth and protest; we swung in philosophical loops, shouting expressive proclamations with newfound words, then landed on solid grammatical ground. Oh, but when we wrote! We picked, smelled, and tasted our words. We relished our combinations and proudly presented our masterpieces.

Then Leslie left me. And I can't help but think that my closeted state contributed to our split. During a class activity with our vocabulary words, I burst into tears. The students were uncomfortable and worried, so I gathered myself and said, "I'm so sorry. I'm dealing with a tragic loss." I dragged myself through April and May, alive in the classroom and a locust shell outside of it.

I thought about ending my life, or at least moving far away— where people didn't know me or my past, where I wouldn't run into Leslie—or any former colleagues from that school. I probably would have done so, but the head of the upper school asked me to fill their English teaching position, offering me the job outright before considering outsiders. My students' parents praised me to the upper-school principal; they were so pleased with what I had done for their children they urged him to hire me.

I was doing some good. I was valued.

And yet, while teaching more sophisticated works, skills, and concepts energized and challenged me, I left an important part of myself outside the campus gates each morning before greeting these teens. Brenda Bock had encouraged me to take the position, but I kept hearing her words when she hired me: "This is a conservative school, and you should not share the details of your personal life."

During my decade as Ms. White, English teacher and varsity soccer coach, I took my ex-husband to a Christmas party; I dated men, trying to escape the anxiety of living as a closeted gay woman.

Then I met Carlton at a bar. Since he lived in Charlotte, I only saw him on weekends, and not every weekend. I did not miss him during the week, and I never enjoyed the occasional sex I felt obligated to have with him. What I did enjoy was casually mentioning to colleagues—and even a class of students—that I was going to a concert with my *boyfriend*. When he showed up at a basketball game, I dramatically jogged to him and hugged him beneath our scoreboard for all to see. As the two of us walked up the bleachers, female students gave me their thumbs up and approving smiles.

That relationship lasted until I kissed a woman with whom I was organizing a 10K Saint Patrick's Day race. And just like that, Carlton was gone, and I was, once again, in a relationship with a woman. Roxanne brought me back from the dead. She was beautiful, intelligent, fascinating, active, kind, and highly skilled in English grammar—which I had learned as we edited our Saint Patrick's Day race brochure.

Nevertheless, I once again refrained from discussing my personal life and avoided public places. In fact, I went out of my way to mention my ex-husband whenever I could, but I never mentioned Roxanne. When Roxanne came to a school play with me, the next day a student asked, "Who was that woman with you?" I shriveled, then said, "She's a friend. Someone who is going through a hard time and needs my help."

I heard from a history teacher that one of my soccer players asked him, "Is Coach White gay?" He assured me that he said "No way!" He meant well, but his fierce denial cast my truth in the wrong.

Another English teacher told me, "A student said, 'Oh my God, I saw Ms. White with her partner at Mamacita's. I was so uncomfortable! They were ordering burritos.' I told her she was wrong—you're not gay." I thanked her for not validating the rumor.

I believed my secrecy would protect me; in fact, those years of living and teaching falsely were self-destructive.

In the spring of 2010, Alex, a student I had taught in ninth-grade English and creative writing, tried to kill himself. I know this because this brave young man, three years after he graduated, spoke to our entire faculty about what it was like to be gay as a student in our conservative school. No one was out, he told us. No students. No faculty members.

As he spoke, I remembered a time I handed the students in his class a short story I'd copied from an anthology. The last page was split with the first page of the next story: E. Annie Proulx's "Brokeback Mountain." Alex asked, "The movie *Brokeback Mountain* is based on a short story?"

I cringed because I had not blacked out that title with a marker before making copies. "Yeah, you'd be surprised at how many short stories have been made into movies," I said, diverting his inquiry to safer ground. I didn't even *think* *a*bout assigning that beautifully written short story. Nor did I tell him how much I appreciated both the story and the movie. Just like the characters in the story, I carefully hid my sexual orientation.

Alex discussed how this curtain of silence made his feelings shameful. When asked what could have helped him, he said, "I knew there were gay faculty members, but they never talked openly about their partners. A picture of a gay teacher's partner on a desk would have made a world of difference to me."

Tears reached my collar, and I fought to stifle an animalistic cry of agony. We gave Alex a standing ovation. I stood in line, waiting to thank him. He smiled at me knowingly. As we hugged, I spoke into his ear, "I am so sorry I hid my identity." He nodded silently, and I walked outside to the brown remains of the school garden and cried for how I had failed Alex and because I was not as brave as this twenty year old.

Did I then put a picture of my partner on my desk? No. Did I ever refer to her in front of students or parents? No. But Alex's honest talk pushed me to be open with my colleagues, even if I continued to avoid the topic of my relationship with my students. I did, however, stop mentioning my ex-husband as a way of tricking them into thinking I was straight, and I did confront students when they made homophobic statements. Little steps.

But then came my leap. Only because I was blindsided.

On Martin Luther King Day, 2014, our administrators decided that instead of having a school holiday, we would meet that day—not for classes—but to celebrate Dr. King's call for justice, peace, and love. We planned age-appropriate activities for students by division. In the upper school, teachers led morning activities before breaking in the afternoon for a speech by Rodney Glasgow (Head of Saint Andrew's Episcopal Middle School in D.C. and Chair of the National Association of Independent Schools' annual Student Diversity Leadership conference) who would then lead us through an exercise in appreciating diversity.

As this dynamic, openly gay black man spoke to us, he stepped out of his clogs and walked around our gym floor, showing off painted toenails that added even more color to the stories he told us of his high-school self, college growth, and clashes with racism and homophobia. The students were mesmerized by his rhetorical richness, his humor, and his honesty. He concluded by stressing how important it is that he, a Harvard graduate with an MFA from Columbia, be proud of all parts of his identity and not hide them—for his accomplishments encourage young people to live comfortably and successfully.

Rodney asked us all to come down to the gym floor and make a large circle alongside the walls. Unlike the morning activities we had planned, faculty members and administrators had no idea where he was leading us. He explained that we all carried multiple identities, and he encouraged us to claim those identities and to respect everyone else's.

I worried. He was not preparing us to tell our favorite foods or to greet someone we didn't know well.

As he wandered around the floor, speaking to us through a microphone about the need for a community to validate others' identities, I felt vulnerable, trapped. I could not leave the circle without drawing unfavorable attention. I braced myself.

"If you identify as a student," he asked, "step inside the circle. Everyone please look around and recognize the students in your community."

"If you identify as a teacher," he continued, "step inside the circle." I stepped forward, anxious. "Everyone please look around and recognize the teachers in your community."

He continued to calmly ask people of different identities to take steps into visibility. I stepped forward for having a learning difference and identifying as white. When the black students stepped forward, I considered how *they* must feel. That feeling stuck as the Asian students stepped forward. Only two of about two hundred people identified as Hispanic. And a lone student rolled his wheelchair forward for people with a physical disability.

"If you identify as a lesbian," Rodney continued, "step inside the circle."

I saw Alex, saw my family, saw my unpainted authenticity. I took three large steps for all the Alexes in the gym. And I trembled with fear and elation to claim me.

I am teaching at the same school, but it is not the same school that hired me. I am not the only faculty member who is openly gay, there are students in same-sex relationships, and we have gender-neutral bathrooms despite North Carolina's virulent HB2 law. I teach a social justice class, and Roxanne, who counsels addicts, was a guest speaker during our unit on mental health and addiction. I proudly introduced her by her profession and as my partner.

Recently, Roxanne and I were looking at jewelry in a downtown shop when a student from my social justice class walked up and said hello to Roxanne, and then to me. As this student told Roxanne how much her presentation meant to her, I rested my hand on Roxanne's warm back.

About the Editors

CANDACE WALSH coedited *Dear John: I Love Jane: Women Write about Leaving Men for Women* (Seal Press, 2010), a Lambda Literary Finalist, with her wife, Laura M. André. She is the author of *Licking the Spoon: A Memoir of Food, Family, and Identity* (Seal Press 2012), a 2013 New Mexico-Arizona Book Awards winner. She also edited the Seal Press anthology *Ask Me About My Divorce: Women Open Up About Moving On*. Her writing has appeared in numerous national and local publications, including *Newsday, Travel +Leisure, Sunset, Mademoiselle, New York* magazine, and *New Mexico Magazine*. She has also worked on staff at Condé Nast International, *Mothering Magazine*, and *New Mexico Magazine* and is currently editor in chief of *El Palacio* magazine. Her essays have been published in various anthologies, on *Slate*, and in the *Huffington Post*. Her screenplay *Birthquake*, cowritten with Laura M. André, was a quarter-finalist in the 2013 Screen Craft Comedy Screenplay Competition.

She is currently enrolled in the Warren Wilson MFA Program for Writers (Fiction) program and frequently teaches writing classes and works one-on-one with writers as a developmental editor. She lives in Santa Fe, NM, with Laura, their two children, and two dogs.

Find out more at candacewalsh.com.

BARBARA STRAUS LODGE is a writer whose personal essays have appeared in *Parabola magazine*; *The Rumpus (Voices of Addiction)*; *Chicken Soup for the Soul*; *The Good Men Project*;

Literary Mama; the *New York Times* "Motherlode" blog; the "LA Affairs" section of the *Los Angeles Times*, and a variety of anthologies. An essay entitled "Mirror Image" written under her pen name Leigh Stuart was published in the anthology *Dear John I Love Jane: Women Write about Leaving Men for Women* (Seal Press, 2010).

She teaches writing to incarcerated young girls through Write-Girl, a Los Angeles-based mentoring program, and is the founder of TruthTalks workshops, offering hope for parents of kids with substance use disorder. She is constantly in awe of her two young-adult children and her loving partner of eight years.

Learn more at barbarastrauslodge.com and truthtalks.us.

About the Contributors

KATE ARCHIBALD-CROSS has written for a variety of newspapers in and around her hometown and currently vows each week to make more time for writing. She is mother to two wonderful sons, partner to one woman of her dreams, and works at a variety of part-time jobs in order to make parenting and household wrangling her first priorities—a financially ludicrous (but emotionally savvy) strategy.

K. ASTRE is a writer with a global appetite for art, music, and culture. She fuels her creativity with tea, yoga, good music, and meditation. She lives with her wife and three children in California.

G. LEV BAUMEL is a writer, traveler, and mother of one delightful daughter. After working with other people's stories for close to two decades—in human rights, print, video, and online—she is now pursuing her own writing career. Baumel is a graduate student, currently getting her MFA with a focus on the power of cross-platform storytelling. She is working on her first book.

TRISH BENDIX is a writer and editor in Los Angeles, California. She is the former editor in chief of AfterEllen.com. Bendix's work has been published in *The Hollywood Reporter*; *Cosmopolitan*; *Slate*; *The Village Voice*; *Time Out Chicago*; *Out*; *Punk Planet*; *Bitch*; The Frisky; AlterNet; and the *Huffington Post*. Her fiction has appeared in *The Q Review* and on CellStories, and she has essays in the 2010 Seal Press anthology, *Dear John, I Love Jane: Women Write about Leaving Men for Women* (Seal Press, 2010); *More Than Marriage* (Ooligan Press); and *Opposing Viewpoints: Celebrity Culture* (Layman Poupard Publishing).

Bendix is the winner of the 2015 Sarah Pettit Memorial Award for the LGBT Journalist of the Year from the National Lesbian and Gay Journalist Association. She is also a board member of the Gay and Lesbian Entertainment Critics Association, and a member of the Television Critics Association as well as the National Lesbian and Gay Journalists Association. She's spoken on panels at SXSW, Q-Me Con, BlogHer, and Creating Change, and to classes at University of Western Washington and Columbia College Chicago.

LOUISE A. BLUM is a novelist, short story writer, and essayist living in Corning, NY. She is the author of the memoir *You're Not from Around Here, Are You? A Lesbian in Small-Town America* (UW Press), and *Amnesty,* a novel from Alyson Publications. She writes about the environment, family, activism, and justice and is currently working on a YA novel called *FRACKED,* about the effects of fracking on one small town in the mountains of rural Pennsylvania.

JEANNOT JONTE BOUCHER is a writer, speaker, and transgender community advocate in Dallas, Texas, as well as a public-school teacher. Jeannot has contributed numerous articles to the *Dallas Morning News, The Male Montessorian,* and *UKEdMagazine.* Boucher is an advocate for transgender students' rights in nondiscrimination policies for bathroom use, while speaking as an openly queer trans public-school teacher and parent. Jeannot and wife, Ashley Boucher, also transgender, speak regularly on university, medical, and LGBT organization panels advocating for trans queer community needs. The pair also perform live music in queerlesque spaces such as Cabaret Boucher. Boucher was named Chamber of Commerce Teacher of the Year in 2014, and has received two awards for innovative teaching.

SHARA CONCEPCIÓN is a Jewyorican writer based in Boston, MA. She received her AA in liberal arts from Borough of Manhattan Community College, her BA in psychology from Smith College, and her MA in gender and cultural studies from Simmons College. Her work has appeared in *Cosmogirl,* Pank Online, and the *Eunoia Review,* and she is a recipient of the City University of New York Undergraduate Poetry award. Though she currently resides in Boston, her heart and its shareholders remain in New York City.

PAT CROW, a fourth-generation Floridian, earned her master's degree in counseling, specializing in marriage and family therapy, in 1989. After practicing and teaching somatic psychotherapy for twenty-five years, she retired and now lives in Santa Fe, New Mexico, where she began writing her memoir about coming out at sixty. She and her partner recently married and share their lives with two diva rescue dogs. She has a daughter living on the west coast, and a son living on the east coast.

RUTH DAVIES lives in Brisbane, Australia, with her partner and cat. Her essay "Marriage Mirage" appeared in *Dear John, I Love Jane: Women Write about Leaving Men for Women* (Seal Press, 2010). She works as an editor of research reports.

VANESSA SHANTI FERNANDO is a writer and social worker living in Vancouver, BC. She still likes reality television. Her recent publications include "Chosen Family," in *Salut King Kong: New English Writing from Quebec* (Vehicule Press, 2015); "Wanting," in *Dear John, I Love Jane: Women Write about Leaving Men* *for Women* (Seal Press, 2010); "The Body, Revolutionary," in *Subversions Journal of Gender & Sexuality* (Concordia University, 2009) and "Vacancy," in *GirlSpoken: From Pen, Brush & Tongue* (Second Story Press, 2007).

KRISTA FRETWELL earns cash to support her writing habit working as a family nurse practitioner in community health. She enjoys Nordic skiing, the dirty parts of gardening, and is an exceptional tree climber. She lives on a small farm in southwestern Washington state with her partner, their five children, two goats, five ducks, four cats, and one big dopey black lab.

ELIZABETH J. GERARD refuses to be boxed in by labels or limitations regarding her life or her work. That refusal, coupled with a deep intellectual curiosity, has led her to attain multiple advanced degrees (Columbia College Chicago: MFA, fiction; Northwestern University: Graduate Certificate, creative nonfiction; University of Chicago: Graduate Certificate, creative writing) as well as diverse training and experience in acting, storytelling, performance poetry, filmmaking, and book and paper arts, among many other interests. She seeks to create art by delving into the darker aspects of life then writing those stories within, across, and in combination of every writing form and genre. She has been published in numerous anthologies, literary journals, and blogs. She has worked as an aquisitions, production, and web editor for *Hair Trigger Student Fiction Anthology*; *Punctuate. A Nonfiction Magazine,* and *The Mini Poetry Chapbook.* Elizabeth continues to work as an assistant editor for *Hotel Amerika* and holds the 2015 CSPA National Gold Award for Best Experimental Fiction—of which she is incredibly proud. She gratefully blames K.B., P.A.M., and A.P. for setting her on this path of being "a real writer."

SHERRY GLASER, actress, playwright, author and commentator, wrote and starred in *Family Secrets*, the longest-running one-woman show in off-Broadway history. In it, Sherry played five members of a typical American family based on her father, mother, two sisters, and grandmother. The show garnered critical acclaim and awards, including the N.Y. Theatre World Award for Best Debut and L.A.'s Ovation Award, as well as rave reviews in the *New York Times* and *Variety*. Simon and Schuster published *Family Secrets: The Book* based on the play. Her essays have been published in a variety of anthologies. Sherry's weekly radio editorials, ongoing engagement in the arenas of politics, humor and spirituality, can be downloaded from her website, sherryglaser.net.

LEAH LAX holds an MFA in creative writing. She's written award-winning fiction and nonfiction, including her memoir excerpted here, *Uncovered: How I Left Hasidic Life and Finally Came Home*. She has also been a finalist for five literary prizes. *Uncovered* has been featured on NPR, the *Advocate*, and the *Huffington Post* and on numerous Best Of and Top Ten lists, and is soon to become an opera by Lori Laitman. When Leah's not writing, you can find her out walking her Airedale or with her wife kayaking around the globe.

JEANETTE LeBLANC spent most of her life working very hard to be a good girl. One day she woke up and decided to write her way out of her own life, and things haven't been the same since. Single mama to two ridiculously unruly daughters, Jeanette believes in the smooth honey bliss of whiskey, the crashing of mama ocean, pencil skirts, vintage band tees and fringed boots, the kinship of the wild wolf, walking for miles in unfamiliar cities, the singular power of dark-red lipstick, the necessity of putting out for the muse on the regular—and that the burn down always precedes the rise. And she believes that sometimes our stories are the only things that can save us. Jeanette writes at peacelovefree.com and is the creator and founder of wildheartwriters.com.

BK LOREN's short fiction and nonfiction can be found in numerous anthologies and periodicals, including *The Best Spiritual Writing* of 2004 and 2012; *Orion Magazine*; *OnEarth* (NRDC's mag); *Parabola*; and many other no-ad magazines. Her novel *Theft* won the Mountains and Plains Independent Booksellers Award and a Willa Award, and was a finalist for the Lambda Novel Award, among others. It is currently optioned for film, with BK writing the screenplay. Her essay collection, *Animal, Mineral, Radical*, won the Colorado Book Award, and many pieces therein garnered national prizes. She lives with her partner in Colorado and is completing a new novel and two screenplays. She invites you to read Sawnie's poetry at sawniemorris.com, because her voice, too, is part of this story. You can reach BK here, if you like: bkloren.com

DARSHANA MAHTANI comes from a Sindhi family. She is a granddaughter to survivors of the Partition of India and Creation of Pakistan. She is currently an ESL Teacher and student of the Raja Yoga practice. She is a poet and an aspiring novelist and screenwriter. She wants to change the world and find the rest of her tribe. She is part of the {R}evolution happening right now, at a corner near you. Recently married to the love of her life, Lauren, they are soon moving to Prescott, AZ, to live out their days in a yurt on a mountain. Learn more about Dolly here: callingonangelsdaily.wordpress.com.

STAR McGILL-GOUDEY is a freelance writer who lives in Tennessee with her husband, children, grandchildren, dogs, horses, and Silkie chickens. She has been published in *Urban Howl*, *Wild Heart Writers*, *Penny Ante Feud*, *Teenage Christian*, and *The Equine Image*. She is on staff at *Wild Heart Writers* as writer and social media minion. She spent most of her life in denial of her bisexuality, but now celebrates who she is. She is committed to being visible and available to those who are on the same path by writing and sharing her journey.

AMANDA MEAD is a writer and teacher in Washington state. She received her MFA from Eastern Washington University, where she served as poetry editor for *Willow Springs*. She has written for *Good Vibrations Magazine* and "i believe you/it's not your fault," and was a contributor to *Dear John, I Love Jane: Women Write about Leaving Men for Women* (Seal Press, 2010). Her poetry has been published in *Calyx, Drunken Boat, Confrontation*, and elsewhere.

CARLA SAMETH has an MFA in creative writing (Latin America) from Queens University and recently completed a memoir-in-essays. Her work has appeared in several anthologies and publications including *Brain, Child*; *Full Grown People*; *Mutha Magazine*; *Narratively*; *Tikkun*; *Pasadena Weekly*, and *La Bloga*.

Carla is a member of the Pasadena Rose Poets, who presented a four-week "Poetry Within Reach" series via an NEA grant in summer 2016. She was a fall 2016 PEN In The Community teaching artist and edited a recently published anthology, *Voices Never Heard*, with writing by her students. She teaches at the Los Angeles Writing Project (LAWP), Secondary Writing Institute at California State University Los Angeles. Carla has helped others tell their stories through her business (iMinds PR), as cofounder of the Pasadena Writing Project and as a writing instructor and mentor for incarcerated youth through WriteGirl.

AMELIA SAUTER is a restaurant owner, professional baker, and freelance food-and-drink writer for a variety of publications, including *Edible Finger Lakes*. She was a contributor to *Dear John, I Love Jane: Women Write about Leaving Men for Women* (Seal Press, 2010), and to the anthology *Here Come the Brides* (Seal Press). She and her wife have chronicled their cancer journey at thebestworstcase.com. Amelia's website (which is actually filled with humor writing) is drinkmywords.com.

JOEY SCHULTZ-EZELL is a fifty-two-year-old woman living in the Kansas City metro area. Her thirty-five-year career has covered the publishing gamut. She was an award-winning sports writer and news reporter before transitioning to the role of editor, then managing editor. She then joined a cutting-edge publishing company where she spent eighteen years as an executive and from which she recently retired. She's written software specs and sports stories, complex patent applications and catchy ad copy, and has published periodicals, books, websites, and marketing materials.

ADA SCOTT received her MFA from Brooklyn College. She has been published in several literary journals, most recently *Rozlyn: Short Fiction by Women Writers*.

EMILY J. SMITH is a writer and tech professional based in Brooklyn. Her writing has appeared in *Salon*; *Bustle*; *Citizens of Culture*; and on Medium.com, among others. You can find her on Twitter @emjsmith.

CASSIE PREMO STEELE, PhD, is the author of fourteen books of poetry, fiction, and nonfiction, including, most recently, *Beautiful Waters*, poetry based on her honeymoon with her wife. Her poetry has been nominated three times for the Pushcart Prize, and she wrote a popular column for *Literary Mama* called "Birthing the Mother Writer." She lives in South Carolina with her wife and daughter, two dogs, and three bunnies.

M. E. TUDOR is originally from central Indiana and now lives in south-central Kentucky with her partner, three grandchildren, three cats, and an adorable dog. She also has two grown daughters who live in southern Kentucky and a total of nine grandchildren, including her partner's three grandchildren. Tudor has lived in Florida, Texas, and Colorado at different times of her life, and her stories reflect her love of traveling, hiking, camping, and being outdoors in general. She is the author of eight novels: *Suddenly*; *The Wrong Place at the Right Time*; *Judge Not*; *Second Chances*; *Afternoon Delight*; *The Perfect Proposal*; *Standing Her Ground* and *Taste Testing* (Tea Rose Books). Find out more at metudor.com.

SUSAN WHITE likes to pretend all of North Carolina is like Asheville. She has been a high-school English teacher for twenty-three years, but only "Teaching Out" for three years. In the gaps between evaluating student writing, she has managed to publish poems, short stories, and creative nonfiction in many publications, including *Dear John, I Love Jane: Women Write about Leaving Men for Women* (Seal Press, 2010); *The Labletter*; *Drunken Boat*; *Pisgah Review*; *The Battered Suitcase* and *Deep South Magazine*. She and her partner share their home with five dogs and two sugar gliders.

EMILY WITHNALL is a writer, teacher, and queer solo parent of two daughters. Her work has appeared in the *Ms. Magazine* blog; *High Country News*; *Mamalode: El Palacio* magazine, and *Concīs Magazine,* among others. An excerpt of Emily's manuscript, *Fracture,* won first place in creative nonfiction for the 2016 AWP Writers' Conferences & Centers Award. Most recently, she was awarded a residency at Sundress Academy for the Arts in 2017 and was a finalist for their VIDA fellowship.

Acknowledgments

We would like to thank Jarred Weisfeld at Cleis Press for getting in touch with Candace out of the blue, just as we were firming up our decision to do a sequel. We would also like to thank every single person who sent us a story. We wish we had had the word count to include them all. Unending appreciation to Krista Lyons, who, when she was at Seal Press, so enthusiastically championed the *Dear John, I Love Jane* proposal and gave us such an amazing debut and such a strong place from which to grow. We also want to thank Lambda Literary, for selecting *Dear John, I Love Jane* as a finalist. Rachel Kramer Bussel generously provided valuable advice. Laura M. André and Louise Smith were unfailingly good natured about being pressed into service as excellent referees and readers. Without all of the vocal and devoted *Dear John, I Love Jane* readers, this book would not have a reason to exist (here's looking at you, Rebecca Gold).

Candace would like to thank Barbara for her saint-level patience, endless enthusiasm, fearless feedback, and for offering her beautiful home as *Janeland* HQ for a dizzy, thrilling, productive launch pad of an editing-marathon weekend that supplemented many hours of virtual meetings and emailed editorial round robins. Barbara will always be her queen for recreating the very essential master Google spreadsheet that mysteriously vaporized one day. She also thanks Mary Anderson for being such an inspiration, cheerleader, and love warrior.

Barbara would like to thank Candace for seeing the value in her submission to *Dear John, I Love Jane* lifetimes ago, which, in fact, launched Barbara's writing career. Candace is, simply put, a force of nature. She gets things done. For Barbara, it has been a unique honor to work with such a beautiful soul who offers boundless inspiration, brilliance, talent, patience, and friendship.

We also want to thank the people and places that shared our call for submissions: Stephanie Lippitt at Cleis Press, Dina Relles at Literary Mama, Susan Maccarelli at Beyond Your Blog, and Jennifer Niesslein at Full Grown People, Facebook friends, secret Facebook groups, and various newsletters.